# A GUIDE TO

# GRAND-JURY MEN,

## DIVIDED INTO TWO BOOKS:

A treatise on the establishment of bills and how to examine the accused during trials of witchcraft in the 15th century. Also detailing a history witchcraft, the methods of discovering witches, and how they may be known, convicted, condemned or punished.

# Richard Bernard

## In Modern Interpretation

### with an Introduction and Notes
### By *Brett R. Warren*

# A Guide to Grand-Jury Men

*From the first and Second Editions.*
*The first, published in 1627. The second, 1629.*

This *Modern Edition* published in 2016
Introduction, annotation, translations and notes
by Brett R. Warren

*Copyright © 2017*

Inquiries may be sent to:
*warr.lancer@gmail.com*

ISBN-13: 978-1542697071

ISBN-10: 1542697077

# Note on Editorial Policy.

This is no mere facsimile of an older publication; the entire work has been completely edited and altered to represent an interpretation of modernity. Most, if not all forms of old/middle English spelling and grammar have been edited into a modern interpretation unless there was no need for the modern reader to further understand its meaning. If misspellings exist, it is due to words no longer being used in today's modern English and the alternatives may take away from intended meaning. Footnotes have been added to provide definitions, citations or further elaborations on the text's emphasis. Names of individuals referenced in the text have been left unaltered to the extent of their intended spelling. No information has been added or taken from the text other than as indicated here and the full text should retain all the same information and value as the original but give greater insight, flow and ease to the modern reader. Translations of various Latin phrases, a variety of definitions, and many other annotations have been included in associated footnotes. The work also includes footnotes from both the first and second editions printed in the 1620's.

- 𝒲

Ætatis suæ 74

Vera Effigies RICH. BERNARD, vigilantif,
simi Pastoris de Batcombe Somfet: Aᵒ 1641:

W. Hollar Bohem, ad vivum del. London.

# Introduction.

A devout Puritan, minister and author of many great religious and biblical works expanding to more than 35 volumes, Richard Bernard was born in Epworth in the year 1568 and went on to obtain his education at Crist's College of Cambridge. He later served through ministry in Batcombe until his death in 1641.

During the mid-17th century, England was plagued by an overwhelming number of deaths and strange sicknesses that affected both men and their cattle. Instances of the demonically possessed caused fear as sightings of spiritual apparitions affected local villages. People tried many methods to cure themselves, some by prayer, by treatments of superstitious rituals or with the help of good witches, healers, and divination. Accusations of witchcraft were increasingly common and a reformation of witch-trial procedure was underway.

Bernard had a practical understanding of sociology and applied the scientific method, as best as any could at the time, to determine whether a person accused of certain criminal acts was truly guilty. He understood that men can be rash and gullible, leading them to quickly make judgements about others when little to no knowledge of the circumstances that directly affected the incident at hand. His research applied philosophical reasoning to better understand the history of witchcraft and the psychological effects of fear in a society ruled by canonical law.

This volume was advisement on how Grand-Jury Men should conduct themselves in cases of witchcraft, along with details on their responsibilities and expected conduct in criminal witch-trials as they examined suspected witches and analyzed instances of bewitchment and maladies that surrounded them. It was first published in 1627 and was influenced by many works and witch-trials from antiquity. The work cites a variety of dissertations and provides a grand historical perspective on the subjects of poison, disease, murders and death believed to have been the cause of witch-craft in the minds of the most learned men of that era but also warns against the punishment of the innocent as many could negligently be falsely accused of witchcraft while explaining how one might know if a suspected witch is truly in league with the devil or just plain trickery.

This present work was his advice on how Grand-Jury Men should conduct themselves in the establishment of a *billa vera (True Bill)* in cases of witchcraft, along with details on their responsibilities and expected conduct in criminal witch-trials. Bernard writes as a minister of Puritan morals and Christian values giving his audience a very valuable history lesson on the ancient perspective of the many problems facing witch-trials from a man living at the time, providing great historical value and knowledge.

# A
# GUIDE TO
# GRAND-JURY MEN,

## DIVIDED INTO TWO BOOKS:

In the *First*, is the Author's best advice to them what to do, before they bring in a *Billa vera* in cases of *Witchcraft*, with a *Christian Direction* to such as are too much given upon every cross to think themselves bewitched.

In the *Second*, is a Treatise touching Witches good and bad, how they may be known, evicted, condemned, with many particulars tending thereunto.

By **RICH. BERNARD**. Of Batcombe

---

### Prov. 17.15.

*He that justifies the wicked, and he that condemns the just; even they both are an abomination to the Lord.*

### Deut. 13.14.

*Thou shalt therefore inquire and make search, and aske, diligently, whether it be truth, and the thing certain,*

---

### LONDON.

Printed by *Felix Kingston* for *Ed. Blackmore*, and are to be sold at his shop at the great South door of *Paul's*.
### 1627.

# TO THE RIGHT

# HONORABLE JUDGES,

Sr. John Walter, *Knight, Lord* chief Baron of his Majesty's Court of Exchequer: and *Sr*. John Den bam, *Knight*, worthy Baron of the same Honorable Court.

The Reverend and Religious Judges in this Western Circuit,

That wisdom from above, with power and courage, be in and upon them from the Lord in all causes before them, to their due praises and endless comfort.

Right worthy Judges,

Since your Lordships sat at *Tanton* the last Summer Assizes, I have (as time and leisure from other studies, and the execution of Divine duties in my function would permit) given myself to the reading of many approved relations touching the arraignment and condemnation of Witches: as also treatises of learned men, concerning the devilish Art of Witchcraft, adding withal not a few things, which otherwise I have learned and observed.

The occasion offered and the reasons drawing me to this study, were the strange fits then, and yet continuing upon some judged to be bewitched by those which were then also condemned and executed for the same: My upright meaning in my painstaking with *Bull* mistaken, a rumor spread, as if I favored Witches, or were of Master *Scot's* erroneous opinion, that Witches were silly deceived Melancholies.[*]

This my labor in all these will clear me: which I am bold to present to your Lordships, as a plain Country Minister's testimony of his hearty rejoicing, that God has sent us such wished-for upright and religious Judges.

I hope it shall not be imputed as evil unto me, that I have chosen such worthily-honored Patrons, so learned in our Lawes, of so great authority in the execution thereof, so judicious in discerning of causes, so just in punishing sin, and so religiously disposed to advance Virtue and Religion.

I do the more herein presume, for that I have observed your Lordships holy attention to the Word delivered before you, and your worthy respect unto God's Ministers; and therefore I doubt not of a favorable acceptance of my best service honestly intended for public good. Yet humbly nevertheless craving pardon, if in anything herein I have taken too much upon me, and to praying heartily for your

---

[*] Reginald Scot published a book titled *The Discoverie of Witchcraft*, a treatise against the persecution of witches.

happy days, and your redoubled honor in your service of God for our King and Country, I humbly take leave.

*Batcombe*. Feb. 24.

*Your Lordships in the tender of his service to be commanded,*

RIC. BERNARD.

# TO THE RIGHT WORSHIPFULL,

Gerard Wood, Doctor of Divinity, and Archdeacon of Wells: and Arthur Duck D. of the Civil Law, & Chan. to the Right Reu. Fa. the L. Bishop of *Bath* and Wells.

Right worshipful,

FOR two books, have I made a double choice of Patrons for protection: because a Treatise of this nature, needs shelter under both, and that which is fortified, am *Ecclesiatico, quàm seculari brachio*,[*] will be more available, and pass more acceptably among all sorts. The sin of witchcraft, and the diabolical practice thereof, is *omnium scelerum atrocissimum*,[†] and in such as have the knowledge of God, the greatest apostasy[‡] from the faith, they renouncing God, and giving themselves by a covenant to the Devil. Bad Witches many prosecute with all eagerness; but Magicians, Necromancers, (of whom his late Majesty gives a deadly censure in his

---

[*] Latin: Ecclesiastical rather than secular.
[†] The most serious of crimes.
[‡] The abandonment or renunciation of a religious or political belief.

*Daemonologie\** ) and the Curing Witch, commonly called, the good Witch, all sorts can let alone: and yet be these in many respects worse than the other. Would God my endeavors might so prevail with men bound by solemn oath, that they would make conscience to present unto you the Ecclesiastical Judges, both the Witches themselves, as also all such as resort unto them. *Impunitas peccandi licentiam peperit.*[†] Yet the evils growing hereupon, both to bodies and souls, cannot sufficiently be expressed. I need not, I hope, with many words entreat your good care to suppress such foul and damnable courses: For I know, that *citò dicta & percipiunt sapiētes, & viris rerū suarum satagentibus non placet urgeri*:[‡] and what need is there *cal car currentibus addere*?[§]

I have heretofore purposed sometime or other to express my due respect unto you both, as being my worshipful good friends. To the one, as justly claiming a thankful remembrance for his so long continued love, and for not a few favors, the true fruits of a good affection: who is to me, *quia filio meo, bengnissimus & incorrupte patronus*, to whom we remain ever obliged. To the other, for so kind and ever loving tenancy, with a readiness, upon any just

---

[*] *Daemonologie*, a dissertation written by King James IV of Scotland and I of England on the study and comparisons of Magic, necromancy, Sorcery, Witchcraft and included a study on Demonology; published in 1591.

[†] The impunity of sin does liberty beget.

[‡] Quickly view and perceive things, and people do not like to be pressed for their assistance.

[§] To add a spur for running.

occasion, to do me any lawful favor. Let it please you now, *eo vuliu sereno, quo meipsum soletis, tractare, hoc qualecun que munusculum accipere*; and shall reckon so favorable in acceptance, as a sufficient recompense for my labor and pains. And so, with due and dutiful respect I take leave,

*Batcombe*. Feb. 26.

*Your Worships at command,*

RIC. BERNARD.

# The sum of these two books

~ The second Book. ~

## CHAP. I.

## CHAP. II.

## CHAP. III.

## CHAP. IV.

## CHAP. V.

## CHAP. VI.

## CHAP. VII.

# CHAP. XXIII.

# A GUIDE TO

# GRANDJURY MEN.

# ~ The first Book. ~

## CHAP. I.

*God's hand is first to be considered in all crosses, whatsoever the means be, and whosoever the instruments: for he rules over all.*

Man, is under the authority of his Maker, who sees all his ways and his wandering bypaths, and to recall him, lays his chastisements upon him: for afflictions come not out of the dust, Job. 5.6. Neither happen they by chance as the *Priests of the Philistines* once spoke, 1. Sam. 6.9. but the evil of punishment is from the Lord, Amos. 3.6.

The Lord smote all the first borne both of man and beast in Egypt, Exod. 21.29. He smote *Jehoram*, the son of *Jehosaphat*, for his Turkish cruelty towards his brethren, with an incurable disease, till his bowels fell out, 2. Chron. 21.18, 19. *Nebuchadnezzar*, Dan. 4.31. by the hand of God upon him, was made brutish, to live like a beast. And did not God's Angel smite Herod,* causing Worms to eat him to death?

Devils does much mischief but even by these also doth God work his will, and these do nothing without the hand of his providence: for,

I. These wicked & unclean spirits, he does send, as the executioners of his justice, as he did amongst the *Egyptians*, Psal. 78. 49. also, between *Abimelech* and the *Sichemites*, Judg. 9.23. So he sent an evil spirit upon Saul to vex him, 1. Sam. 16. 15. and a lying spirit into the mouths of the false *prophets*, 1. King. 22. And it is plain in Saint *Mark* that the Devils desired Christ to send them into the herd of Swine, Mar. 5.12.

II. When he has sent them, they do not what they list, but proceed so far only, as he pleases, whether to hurt a man's body, or his children, or his goods: they are strictly limited, and cannot go beyond their commission, as may be seen in the story of Job, 1.12. and 2.6. Yea, though they be not a few, but a very *Legion of devils*, they cannot enter into the Swine of the filthy *Gadarenes*,† without God's leave and license, Matthew 8.31.

---

* Acts 12.23.

† The Country of the Gadarenes is mentioned in a great many manuscripts of the New Testament but comes from *Gergesenes* which literally means "*those who come from*

III. As they cannot do what they will, so they cannot stay to vex or afflict any, longer then he pleases: for he can bind the Devil by his Angels, Reu. 20.1. he can give man power over them, Mar. 6.7. and when he commanded, they must give over, though never so sore against their wills, Luk. 4.35.

If he thus rules over Devils, we may well think that he has a hand over his instruments, Witches and Sorcerers. He gave the Magicians and Sorcerers of Egypt, leave for a while to work their feats: but when he pleased, he restrained them, and then they could do no more, Exod. 8.19. And did not the Witch *Balaam* confess, saying, Though *Balak* would give him his house full of gold and silver, he could not go beyond the Word of the Lord, to do less, or more, Num. 12.18. although *Balak* thought otherwise, that *Balaam* could bless & curse whom he lifted: But if God does not cure, a Witches curse is of no force, Num. 23.8. *Elymas* was a famous Sorcerer: but how quickly did God confound him by the Ministry of *Paul*, and struck him blind, before the Deputy and the people, Act. 13.11? Neither Devils, nor Witches, nor wicked men, can do anything without the Lord's leave, Gen. 19.11. & 31. 29. Isa. 37.29.

These things being so, the consideration hereof should teach men:

---

*pilgrimage or fight"*. Both Gerada and Gerasa were cities located towards the east of both the River Jordan and the Sea of Galilee. Today, it is known as Gergesa.

I. To take heed, not to provoke God to wrath, who is the God of hosts: who has his Angels in heaven to send out against us, the powers of all his creatures to punish us: as the fire to consume us, as he did *Sodom*: the waters to drown us, as he did the *Egyptians*: the earth to open and swallow us up, as it did the Rebel *Corah* and his company. The wicked of the world can he make to rise up, and to kill one another, 2. Chr. 20.23. Yea, he has Devils at command to go out and torment men, 1. Sam. 16.15. and he can let them loose to work for Witches, that they may have their desires upon the wicked, to make men always fear and tremble before him.

II. Being afflicted, not to curse or blaspheme, as Satan labors to make men do,[*] and as the wicked will do; nor to be furiously enraged against suspected instruments, as vain, dissolute, and irreligious people commonly do, which desire forth with to be revenged on them, as if it were those only that afflicted them: But first, men ought with all reverence and fear, to acknowledge, that all that befalls them, to be God's hand: yea, though they know, the Devil and his devilish instruments, to have their hands therein. *Job* in his trouble said, *The Lord giveth, and the Lord taketh away*, Job. 1.12. His terrors, he called them the *terrors of God*, Chap. 6.4. and he said, that *God scarred him with dreams, and terrified him with visions*, Chap. 7. 14. *Joseph* in his troubles, yea, in his brethren's unnatural dealings, saw the Lord therein, Gen. 45.5, 7. and said it was not they, but the

---

[*] Job 1.11 & 2.5. Reu. 16.11. Scot Disc. of Witch. p. 1.2

Lord, that sent him into *Egypt*. Yea, the Church in her great calamities, though she saw the instruments and felt there wrath, yet she says, that God had done these things, Lam. 1.15. & 2. 1, 7. And this acknowledgement is sometimes in the mouths of very Witches, confessing, that the evil befalling them and others, is the very finger of God, Exo. 8.19. And so, said Saul's servants of the evil spirit: *That he was sent of the Lord upon* Saul *to vex him*, 1. Sam. 16.15.

2. Therefore to be patient towards the instruments, as was *David* towards *Shimei*, who threw stones at him, railed on him, and cursed him: 2. Sam. 16.10. He yet held his peace, because he knew the Lords will was therein, and that he had done it, Psa. 39.9. We may not be like to *Jehoram* the son of a *Jezabel*, who though he knew, that the Lords hand was upon him and his people, and also did acknowledge so much, yet was he so impatient to endure the misery, and so hellishly enraged, as he swore to be revenged upon *Elisha* the Prophet, and to take away his life, 2. King. 6.31, 33. as if he had been the cause of their calamity. True it is, that evil instruments are to be punished, and our patience should not hinder nor hold back the course of Justice: but this is not to be looked unto in the first place, nor, the instruments to be pursued with wrath and with a revengeful spirit, as if they were only to be blamed, and not men themselves for their sins, procuring such evils to themselves.

3. Seeing God's hand upon us (who doth not willingly grieve us, if we provoke him not, Lam. 3.33. Jer. 25.6.) this must draw us to a searching of our

5

ways, Lam. 3.40. to the acknowledgement of our sins,[*] and to confess God to be just: and so humble ourselves in fasting and prayer, leaving our ill courses, and laboring to be reformed, and so remove God's hand. And afterwards, if there be evident proof, and just cause, then to proceed; Yet with charity, against wicked instruments, seeking to have them punished, for their amendment. This is Religion: this is Christian-like: thus, ought the afflicted to behave themselves, and not swear & stare, curse and rage, against such as they suspect to harm them, seeking to be revenged of them, plotting their deaths, and rejoicing that they have their wills, and so think all to be well: though their ways be wicked, going on still without reformation, even to the pit.

And as the afflicted should be humbled under God's hand, so the beholders looking on their afflictions, should not sit down to censure them, because they suffer such things; as *Job's* friends did to him; but should learn Christ's lesson, thereby to see their own danger, and know, that except they repent, they may likewise be so tormented, and perish, Luk. 13. 3, 5.

---

[*] 2. Chr. 12.6.

# CHAP. 2.

*Strange diseases may happen either to man or beast, and the same originally from some natural cause, and neither effected by Devils, nor yet proceed from Witches.*

IT is the general madness of people to ascribe unto Witchcraft, whatsoever falls out unknown, or strange to vulgar sense. I will here therefore write down the particular instances of strange and wonderful diseases set down by a learned Physician; [*] in all which is a deceiving appearance, coming near to the similitude of bewitching, in ordinary and common apprehensions which cannot discern of diseases, nor the true causes thereof. I will here write them out, as I find them in his discourse, yet a little more distinctly, for common capacities. [†]

In one kind of disease (he calls it *Catalepsis* or *Catoche*) the whole body is as it were in a minute suddenly taken in the midst of some ordinary gesture or action (whether sitting, standing, writing, or

---

[*] Doctor. Cotta in his discourse of Emperucks. and chap. 8 of Witchcraft.
[†] *Catalepsis.*

looking up to the heavens, as another Physician speaks * ) and therein is continued some space together, as if frozen, generally stark and stiff, in all parts without sense or motion; yet with the eyes open and breathing freely, as if the party were a living image. What common conceit beholding this (as it be fell to a child of one Master *Bakers* of *Coventry*, who was thus afflicted,) but would think there were Witchcraft here practiced?

In another disease, (as in the Apoplexia, or in *morbo attonito*,[†] as he speaks) the sick are also suddenly taken and surprised with a senseless trance and general astonishment, or sideration[‡] and benumbing of all the limbs, void of all sense and moving, many hours together, only the breath strives against the danger of suffocation, and still the pulse beats.

In another,[§] the sick are swiftly surprised with so profound and deadly asleep, as no call, nor cry, nor noise, no stimulation can in many hours, awake and raise them. So was one Master *Rosin* of *Northampton* taken for the space of two days, and two nights.

---

* Doctor. Mason in his pract. of Phys. part 1. c. 12. Sect. 11. sol. 136.

[†] *Apoplexia – in modern use,* apoplexy - the sudden loss of consciousness caused when a rupture of a blood vessel restricts oxygen pathways to the brain.

[‡] Meaning *sedation*.

[§] The *Carum*.

*Julius* the 2. Pope of that name, was thus afflicted, and Joannes Scotus (as another writes) * lying, by this sickness, as dead, was buried before he was dead.

In another (by *Galen* (says he) called *Coma vigilans*)† the sick are doubtfully held,‡ in some part waking, in another part sleeping: in some respects, manners and parts, expressing wakeful motions; sense, speech, right apprehension, memory and imagination: but in other respects, parts and manners, as asleep, void of the liberty and use of sense, motion, or any other faculty.

Now contrary to these former, he makes mention of diverse others, as of the falling sickness, and of divers kinds of convulsions: In these diseases,

1. Some will bite their tongues, and flesh.

2. Some make fearful and frightful outcries and shrieking.

3 Some are violently tossed and tumbled from one place to another.

4. Some froth, gnash with their teeth, with their faces deformed, and drawn awry.

---

* Bodin. in *Daemonomaenia*, lib. 2. c. 6.
† Waking coma – when individuals are comatose, in a state of unconsciousness and unable to awake regardless of any applicable stimuli.
‡ *Coma vigilans*

9

5. Some have all parts pestered, and writhed into ugly shapes: as their heads forward, their faces backward, eyes rolling, inordinately twinkling, the mouth distorted into divers forms, grinning, mowing, gaping wide, or close shut.

6. Some have their limbs, and divers members suddenly with violence snatched up and carried aloft, and by their own weight suffered to fall again.

7. Some have an inordinate leaping, and hopping of the flesh, through every member of the body, as if some living thing were there.

And as the body is metamorphosed into such strange shapes, so in some diseases (says he) is the mind strangely transported into visions and apparitions:[*] so as sometimes they will complain of Witches and Devils, broadly describing the shapes and gestures of such as are coming towards them.

One example amongst many other, he brings of a Gentleman's daughter in *Warwickshire*, his patient, afflicted in an unknown manner, & strange, to her parents, neighbors, and to some Physicians also.

1. She had a vehement shaking, and violent casting forward of her head every day *at a set time*, in a much-marveled fashion, and indeed with a loud and shrill inarticulate sound of two syllables *Ipha Ipha*.

---

[*] Note this.

2. She had diverse tortures of her mouth and face, with staring and rolling her eyes, sprawling and tumbling upon the ground, grating and gnashing of her teeth.

3. Sometimes she fell into a deadly trance, therein continuing the space of a day, representing the shape and image of death, without all sense and motion, saving breathing and her pulse, neither was she moved with pinching, or the like.

4. When she came out of the same, she would, as if fearfully affrighted, cast her eyes looking backward, then on either side, and over her head, as seeing something, and then her eyes would be staring open, and her mouth gaping wide, with her hands & arms strongly stretched out above her head, with a general starkness and stiffness.

5. When she was out of her fits and seemed to sleep and slumber, then her imagination led her hands to divers actions and motions, arguing folly, and defect of reason, with her hands only feeling (without the help of any other sense) she would dress and attire the heads of such women, as were by her, so strong was her imagination to lead her feeling.

These and other particulars are mentioned; yet the causes natural, and natural means were used by him, and at length by the benefit of the *Baths* she was cured.

11

*Another story he records of a poor boy of Pichley in Northampton shire, who was suddenly surprised with a vehement confusion, drawing his head and heels violently backward, carrying his whole body into a roundness, tumbling up and down, with much pain and inward groaning. The parents held him bewitched, and therefore sent for a wise woman, who played her witchery tricks, but could do nothing. The Doctor showed the natural cause to be Worms, which in some time after, the Boy did void, and was perfectly well▪

In another book of his, called *The Tryall of Witchcraft*, chap. 2. pag. 15, 16, 17. he makes mention of divers sorts of persons tormented with diseases, with their terrible accidents and afflictions to the body, of men, women and children, the reason whereof could not be discerned till after death: but their bodies being opened, the reasons in nature, were very evident in sight.

Amongst the rest, one story he relates, to show the pestilent evil of seeking to a *white Witch and Wizard*, of a *Gentle woman* strangely afflicted, with variety of strange tormenting diseases together; and being almost cured, it was by a *Wizard* whispered, and thereupon besleeved, that she was merely bewitched: which supposed Witches were thereupon attached, accused, arraigned, found guilty and executed; and yet (says he) in true reason, and judicious discerning, it is as clear, as the brightest day, that no accident

---

* In the same book, c. 9

befalling her, was other than natural. An accursed crediting then of a Wizard, unjustly occasioned the taking away of the lives of these so suspected; But though the diseases ceased for some six years, yet some of her fits returned again in the seventh year following, and continued longer upon her, then the other; and now if they will believe a Wizard again, they must go & conceit other Witches, and hang them too.

But now to leave diseases, it is good to observe the force of *Fancy* and *Fear*,[*] whereby may be found Witches. But where? only in a foolish sconce (as he speaks.) And to show this, he instances the force thereof in two women going to a Physician, one after another.[†] To the one he said, she was like to be vexed with the *Sciatica*,[‡] whereof he saw the apparent signs, which she affirmed never to have had the motion of in all her life: now the same night returning home, she was painfully and grievously afflicted with it. To the other, coming some two or three days after, besides the pain she made known, he by signs told her of the Cramp, which she before sensibly never had felt, yet that night also it came to her.

Now the first party knowing how it happened to herself, and hearing the like of her neighbor,

---

[*] In his book against Empirics, c.8.

[†] Instances in two women.

[‡] *Sciatica* is a medical condition usually caused by a compressed nerve of the spinal cord during the degradation of a disk in the invertebrate. Symptoms include pain in the outer leg, hip or back

presently concluded, that she surely was bewitched by the Physician. But after her husband, (an understanding man) to satisfy his wife's mind being impatient during her pains) had gone and returned from the Physician, she was altered in her opinion, and then prayed her husband to go once more to ask him forgiveness, and if he so would, then should she be well, and indeed so her imagination wrought, that at her husband's return, she met him at the door, and told him that she was well.

How did a lusty young man at the Assizes presently faint in reading a conference of two spirits, whilst the suspected Witch was at the Barre, merely upon fear to be in danger to be bewitched, as was evident by his words, saying, *O thou Rogue, wilt thou bewitch me too?*

Fear and imagination make many Witches among country people, being superstitiously addicted, and led with foolish observations, and imaginary signs of good and bad luck.

Therefore, seeing there may be such natural causes truly alleged for those things, which seemed to be inflicted by Satan, and the provocation of Witches:

I. Let such as suspect themselves to be bewitched, consider whether the cause of their vexation be not natural and enquire not of a devilish Wizard, but of learned and judicious Physicians to know their disease, lest they suspect their neighbors unjustly, and for a just punishment, God give them over into the hands of those that they do fear. So likewise should they in the loss of their cattle, look to the natural causes of their death: for a beast and horse may die suddenly, and not be bewitched; as an horse of one Master *Dorington* in *Huntington shire*, * suddenly falling down dead, was opened, there was found in his heart a strange worm round together like a Toad, but being spread, had 50. branches, and was seventeen inches long.

II. The Gentlemen of the *Grand-Jury*, in case of Witchcraft, when complaints are made; should

1. Be requisitive of the grounds leading the Complainant, why he thinks himself, or any of his, to be bewitched? whether it be not rather from his own fear, then from any other cause? or whether the affliction be not from some natural cause?

2. To inquire whether he has taken advice of some learned Physicians, and has also used their best helps, for remedy, before they enter into consideration of the practices of Witchery: because unless the Witchcraft be very clear, they may be much mistaken; and better it were, till the truth appear, to write an *Ignoramus*,† then upon oath to set down *Billa vera*, and so thrust an intricate case upon a Jury of simple men, who proceed too often upon relations of mere

---

* Howes Chron. sol. 19.

† An ignorant person.

presumptions, and these sometimes very weak ones too, to take away men's lives.

It is undoubtedly true, that there is a very great likeness, and also a deceivable likeness, between some diseases natural, and those that be really and truly supernatural, coming by the Devil and Witchery, and therefore need the judgment of some skillful Physician to help to discern, and to make a clear difference between the one and the other, that men may proceed judiciously, and so rightly with comfort of conscience, that they be not guilty of blood.

Sometimes with a natural disease Satan may also intermix his supernatural work, to hide his, and the Witches practices, under such natural diseases, when they at one time work together. This requires great understanding, to make a true decision, and right distinction of one from the other, by reason of the illusion (as one says) of their deceivable likenesses.

But though to the simple, the likeness between both may seem one and the same, yet the truth is, the Devil cannot so mix his work with a natural disease,[*] but the same may be detected in the manifest odds, and that in two things very clearly, as I have read out of a learned Physician.

I. By the *Symptoms* and effects, which show themselves beyond the nature of the disease. The

---

[*] See *Delrio in Disq. mag. lib.* 6. cap. 2. Sec. 2. q. 3. pag. 967.

natural disease, with the true causes, and proper effects being first known, the other effects must needs be from the secret working of some supernatural power.[*] As for example in a *Convulsion* (with which a Noble *young man* was extraordinarily for a long time tormented) according to the ordinary causes thereof in nature, it bereaves the Patient of motion: for his limbs are stark and stiff: also it deprives him of sense and understanding. Therefore, in a *Convulsion* to have (as the young man had) an incredible swiftness of motion, and withal understanding and sense perfect, it must needs be supernatural.

II. By natural remedies discreetly and fitly applied according to Art: for there are two ways by these, to detect the finger of Satan.

1. When these natural means do lose their manifestly known nature, and certainly approves use and operation always in their due application to the disease, whereto they properly belong.

2. Withal, when the use of these remedies does produce effects clean contrary to their proper and natural operation: as when one labors of a vehement burning thirst, and shall receive some most and cooling thing to allay the heat, the same shall not only lose his nature, but also cause a greater thirst immediately, and withal the hard closing up the

---

[*] Fernel. hib. 2. cap. 16. de abditis rerum causis (The hidden causes).

mouth thereupon. This must needs be supernatural. This second is to be added to the former, because medicines may, for want of God's blessing, lose their operation, and because that God will perhaps have sometime the disease to be incurable.

# CHAP. III.

## *The supposed to be bewitched and tormented by the Devil, may be very counterfeit.*

There may be neither any natural disease, nor any supernatural work of the Devil in the seemingly afflicted party: but a mere counterfeiting of actions, motions, passions, distortions, perturbations, agitations, writhing, tumbling, tossing, wallowing, foaming, alteration of speech and voice, with ghastly staring with the eyes, trances and relation of visions afterwards. For there is nothing almost in things of this nature so really true, but some can so likely resemble the same, as the spectators shall judge the parties to be so indeed, as they seem to be in outward appearance.

\* There was one *Marwood*, a confederate with *Weston*, *Dibdale*, and other Popish Priests,† who did so cunningly act his part, in trembling, foaming, and raging, when he was touched with Campions girdle,

---

\* See *the Declaration of Popish imposture*.

† *Papist* is a religious slur to label Roman Catholics as their loyalties are seen to be with the papacy (meaning the heads of the Catholic Church) of Rome. A Popish is simply a term meant to identify a Roman Catholic.

forsooth, as made the gull'd lookers on to weep, in beholding the cogging and juggling companion in such a seeming miserable plight. The like I saw of a lewd girl at *Wells*; who to be revenged of a poor Woman, which had justly complained against her to her Mistress, counterfeited to be bewitched by her, and so played her part, as she made many to wonder, and some to weep, as if she had been possessed.

*The Boy of *Bilson* his counterfeiting discovered, is notorious throughout the land; which Boy seemed to be bewitched, and cried out of a woman to have bewitched him and when she was brought in very secretly, he could discern it. He had strange fits, and seemed therein deaf and dumb he could writhe his mouth aside, roll his eyes, as nothing but the white would appear, and his head shake as one distracted. He usually would cast up his meat, vomit pins, rags, straw, wrest and turn his head backward, grate with his teeth, gape hideously with his mouth, cling and draw in his belly and guts; groan and mourn piteously; tell of the apparition of a spirit after his fits, seeming like a black bird. He made water like ink sometimes, which some tried, and wrote with it. At the mentioning of the beginning of Saint *John's* Gospel: *In the beginning was the Word*, etc. he would fall into his fits, as if he could not endure to hear these words: He became with fasting very weak, and his limbs by enduring extremities, were benumbed. And to conclude, so resolved was he to bear out his counterfeiting, as when he was pinched often with

---

* The Boy of Bilson.

fingers, pricked with needles, tickled on the sides, and once whipped with a rod (being but thirteen years old) he could not be discerned by either shrinking, or shrieking, to bewray the least passion or feeling.

And yet was he discovered to be a counterfeit, and openly confessed the same, and bow he came to learn these tricks, and by whom, and wherefore. At the Assizes, he cried God mercy, craved pardon of the poor Woman; and lastly, prayed the whole Country to admit of his hearty confession and satisfaction.

To this may be added another example delivered by Master *Scot*, in his *discouerie of Witchcraft*, book 7. chap. 1. and 2. The story is of one Mildred a Bastard of one *Alice Norrington*, servant to one *William Spooner* of *Westwell* in *Kent*; *Anno* 1574. She feigned the voice of a Devil within her, distinct from her own voice. This counterfeit Devil made answer to a great number of questions propounded by Ministers: He named one old woman for a Witch, one old *Alice*, who kept him twenty years in two bottles, on the back side of her house, and elsewhere, and that he came in the likeness of two birds, and was called *Partener*, and that at her instigation he had killed three, and named who they were, with many other things: Of all which, there were many witnesses, the names set down by Master *Scot*, and yet all this was counterfeited, and found out by one Master *Wotton*, and one Master *Darrel*, Justices, she confessed, and for the same received due punishment.

In this strange counterfeiting, it may yet verily be thought, that Satan might therein help him and her to play so cunningly this part as they did: for Satan is ever ready to further wickedness, especially tending to the shedding of blood, and to further Popish Idolatry, which the Boy of *Bilson* was enticed to do, and the Popish Priests sought for to establish, in exorcising the Boy, and professing to dispossess him of three Devils, if his parents would turn, forsooth, Catholics.

Did not our late King *James*, by his wisdom, learning, and experience, discover divers counterfeits?

Of *Jugglers*, and their quick conveyances; as also of *Tumbler's* dexterity, agility and vivacity of spirit, what they can do even to work admirations as also of *feigning a voice* and *hollow speaking*, even to deceive the sharpest apprehension: Let such as please, read *Peter de Loier de spectris*, translated by *Zacharie Jones, cap.*8.

Of a counterfeit *Demoniac*, one for many is *Martha Brosier*, a French woman, * of whom a large discourse is written by the Physicians of Paris to the King of France.

This young woman of some two and twenty years of age, had many Spectators, Bishops, Abbots, Ecclesiastical persons, Divines, Religious men, Counselors of State, Advocates, Gentlemen, ladies

---

* Martha Brosier.

and Gentlewoman, with many learned Physicians, mentioned in the discourse.

She would fetch her breath very short, put her tongue out very far, gnash with her teeth, writhe her mouth, as if she had a convulsion, roll and turn her eyes, disfigure her face, with divers foul, unseemly and deformed looks, seem now and then to be vexed and tormented with many different and furious motions of all the visible parts of her body. There was a rumbling noise, like the spleen under her short ribs, on the left side, and her flank she would shake as a panting horse after a violent race; often she would utter a roaring voice, when some read these words; *Verbum caro factus est, & homo factus est:*[*] then with all her strength she would play her gambols: sometimes lying upon her back, she would as it were skip, and at four or five such lifts, she would remove herself a great way, as once from an Altar, to the door of a great *Chapel*, to the astonishment of the beholders, as if a very devil had carried her: And though her motions were violent and sudden, yet there seemed no change of pulse, breath, or color. In her fits, she would endure without show of pain, the deep pricking of pins in her hands, and neck, and hardly any sign of blood. And yet for all these things, after diverse months she was wisely discovered to be a lewd counterfeit, and so adjudged by the Parliament, & that judgment maintained for sound by the learned Physicians of *Paris*, as is to be seen in the published discourse, wherein they give reasons

---

[*] Latin: The Word was made flesh, and was made man.

of these her practices. And whereas it was reported that she spoke in her belly and breast,[*] when her mouth and lips were shut, they show, that it is no argument to prove a Devil to be such an one, and do bring two instances; one of a *woman* (as *Mildred* before mentioned) that could do so; and another of a *Rogue*, as they call him, who by this trick and such other devices got much money.

Now of these counterfeits, some play their parts for gains, as the last named: *some* for revenge, as the Wench at *Wels*: *some* to advance Popery, as did *Marwood*: *some* to please others, which would have it so,[†] as one *Mairo* another companion with *Westen* and *Dibdale*, did in feigning his trances, though he was indeed no counterfeit in his disease, (called *hysterica passio*)[‡] but his trances he confessed to be feigned: *some* of a pleasure they take to gull spectators, and to be had in admiration, when they perceive their feats and devised tricks to get credit, and by relation to be made much more then they be,

---

[*] To speak in the breast or belly, with the mouth closed shut.

[†] In the Declaration of Popish imposture.

[‡] Hysterical passion –

"From ancient times through the nineteenth century, women suffering variously from choking, feelings of suffocation, partial paralysis, convulsions similar to those of epilepsy, aphasia, numbness, and lethargy were said to be ill of hysteria, caused by a wandering womb." - Coppélia Kahn

This hysterical passion was a medical condition thought only to affect women and was a common phrase used by physicians in antiquity. It was used in Shakespeare's *King Lear* to describe his inability to control his emotions, a trait amongst women.

as the many false reports went of the aforesaid *Martha*, that she was lift up into the air, and, that she spoke Greek and Latin, and other things, which she never did.

For when people come to see such supposed to be possessed by a Devil or Devils; some are filled with fanciful imaginations, some are possessed with fear; so, as they at first time on a sudden, think they hear and see more than they do, and so make very strange relations without truth, if they take not time, & come again, and again, to see and consider with judgment, and with mature deliberation such deceivable resemblances.

Therefore, here the Gentlemen of the *Grand Jury*, before they write *Billa vera*, are with all serious attention to look upon the seeming bewitched, and to ponder all the circumstances, lest they be deceived by a counterfeit: for such a one, without very wary circumspection, may soon be taken for one indeed bewitched, and that upon these grounds:

1. Through men's sudden beholding such unaccustomed strange feats, as these counterfeits can act.

2. By their simple apprehension of the outward appearances of things, not imagining that therein is deceit.

3. He upon their easy belief, to take it as they see and imagine also to be, without diligent search to dive farther into the deceit.

4. By the relation of that that they have seen & heard, with not a few additions of their own mistake, setting all out with words of wonderment, to allure others to their vain beliefs.

5. Lastly, by the credulousness of too, too many, receiving these reports as true, and over-confidently averring them so to be to the settling of men's opinions, that those shows are indeed substances, and that the party, or parties are bewitched, without all peradventure.

Therefore, let the wise Jury here make diligent inquiry,

1. After the wisdom and discretion of the witnesses, whether they can discern well between real and counterfeit acts; and how they so discern the same.

2. What sufficient trial has been made of the supposed bewitched, as also, by whom, and how long.

3. And to these let them ad, for still better satisfaction, their own endeavors, to discover the juggling tricks.

*But here it may be demanded, How Counterfeits may be discovered?*

†To answer to this, we must consider, first, what a Counterfeit is, and secondly, what it is that he endeavors to counterfeit.

1. A *Counterfeit* is not that truly, which he pretends to be, but only a shadow thereof in a most cunning manner, resembling it, that by the likeness be may deceive others, to further his own intended ends therein: so that in the resemblance & apparent shows lies the deceit. To this, the spectators must diligently take heed, observe warily, set themselves down to examine them afterwards, and to be careful not to credit anything at first view.

A *Counterfeit* is not restrained by the power of that which he or she labors to shadow out, whether a thing natural, or supernatural; which in one, not a Counterfeit, have a power over him or her, in whom, or on whom they be; so as they cannot show them at their own pleasure, but when the natural, or supernatural power works: but the *Counterfeit* is his own, to do his tricks when he pleases, for his best advantage.

Therefore the judicious Spectators, are to weigh seriously the occasion of entering into the fits, with all circumstances, before whom, at what time, in

---

* Quest.
† Answ.

what place, who those be which are about him or her, what both the party and they do before, in the time of the fit, and after; and withal, to observe the manner how the party enters, continues, and ends the fits: that out of either some, or out of all these, his or her fraud may be discovered, as undoubtedly it may in convenient time, though not on a sudden, not in the concourse of an ignorant, wondering, talking, and amazed multitude, necessarily to be removed, in trying a cunning Counterfeit.

II. Having thus considered the first thing for the discovery, the next is, to know what he goes about to counterfeit, not professedly, as Stage-Players do, the actions, manners, conditions, places, and states of men; but one of these two, either the *natural* (but violent) *diseases*, or *supernatural works* of the Devil.

If he or she counterfeit natural diseases, as the *Apoplexy*, the *Epilepsy*, the *Convulsion*, the *Frenzy*, *Histerica passio*, the *Suffocation* of the *Matrix*,* or the *Mother*, the motion of *Trembling* and *Panting*,† the *Cramp* and *Stiffness*, or the diseases mingled of these, the learned, judicious and experienced

---

* The *Suffocation of the Matrix* is also called, *fits of the mother*. The word *matrix* is actually taken from the Latin for *matris*, meaning mother. Hence, this matrix is a medical term from antiquity to mean *the mother's womb*. The symptoms derive from an impendent of various bodily actions, especially the bodily respiratory functions. This is not a term used by modern physicians and the cause at the time was not yet known.
† How to discover a Counterfeit of natural diseases.

Physicians must discover him or her so counterfeiting.

But in absence of these, for the present, if any be otherwise learned, and have books, let him or them,

I. Consider the nature of any disease, and the accidents thereof, which is to have their times of beginning, of increasing, of full force, and so of declination.

Now this being so, the nature of natural diseases and accidents thereof, as Physicians do teach: enquiry must be made, whether they began by little and little, increasing in time to full force: or that at the first, when they seemed to take beginning, they at once then mounted to the utmost extremity; and do likewise cease all in a moment: then the disease and accidents thereof, are either counterfeit, or supernatural, as were the Boyles on the *Egyptians*,[*] and blains suddenly breaking out, as did the sore boils on *Job's* body, and were not natural.

II. Consider the fits and to what special disease those fits may be resembled: and if any have such books, as do describe: the nature of such, diseases, let them look thereinto, and compare them together to see the odds and differences between them.

III. Consider how that natural diseases and motions thereof especially violent ▪ (which these undertake to

---

[*] Exo. 9. Job. 1.7.

counterfeit) leave the bodies weakened, the visage pale, the breath panting, the pulse; changed the spirits enfeebled, with such other effects, as violent diseases, from natural causes do produce, and leave as true testimonies of the truth thereof. If therefore after the violent fits, the parties be strong, can walk about, talk with merry company, toss the pot, whiff the Tobacco pipe and such like; the disease, if it be not supernatural, it is counterfeit; for it is not natural.

But before I leave this; one thing more may be noted, that even a Counterfeit may have some natural disease upon him or her, and make advantage thereof, adding their own juggling tricks thereto. As *Mahomet*,* the *Turkish* false prophet made benefit of the falling sickness, with which disease he was afflicted. So some with melancholy affected, may become pale and meager, and being subtle in their intention, will thereof make use to play their pranks. Many before named, had the *Hysterica passio*, and added thereto counterfeit trances. Care therefore must be had, to difference the counterfeiting, from that which is natural, which requires judgment. And therefore, albeit, I have set down these, as some helps, where the Physician cannot be had, to inform the Gentlemen of the Jury; yet if it be possible, let them use the learned men's help and advice in these things. And thus much for the discovering of a counterfeit in natural diseases.

---

*

*But now if he or she counterfeit. Diabolical practices of persons bewitched and possessed; then are the Gentlemen to acquaint themselves with the true signs of such as be possessed, so to discover the dissembler; and according as I find in holy Scripture, they be these:

I. An extraordinary strength, accompanied with exceeding fierceness, to be able to pull chains in sunder, and to break fetters in pieces, to cut themselves with stones, to tear off their clothes, & to go naked; to run into solitary and hideous places, and not to be tamed: Here is a Devil, Mar. 5.4.5. Luk. 8.29.

II. When one is suddenly taken up, and thrown with violence among and in the midst of a company, and not be hurt, Luke. 4.35.

III. When one is *Lunatic*, taken often and cast into the fire, or water to be destroyed, Math. 17.15 Mar 9 22.

IV. When one wallows, foams, gnashes with his teeth, is rent and thrown to and from, and withal *pines* away in body, as in Mar. 9.18, 20. and that for a very long time, to be so tormented.

V. When sight, hearing, and speech, is taken from one strangely, as in Math. 12.22. Mar. 9.25.

---

* *How to detect a Counterfeiter* of diabol and supernanu. tricks.

VI. When one is violently tormented, the spirit bruising the party, making him or her, with tearing to foam again, and suddenly to cry out, Luk. 9.39.

VII. When one speaks, in his or her fits, in an extraordinary manner, not after their own natural or ordinary course of understanding, as did Saul, 1. Sam. 18.10. speaking such truths, as possible they by no natural apprehension, or by instruction, could attain unto, as did divers possessed, concerning Christ, who, they said, was *the holy one of God*. Mar. 1.24. *The Son of God*, Mar. 3.11. *The Son of the most high God*, Mar. 5.7. and as the *Pythoness* said of *Paul* and *Sylas, These are the servants of the ever living God, and teach unto you the way of Salvation*, Act. 16. This knowledge they had not by natural reason: for flesh & blood revealed it not, Mat. 16 Neither did they learn it of men: for the Jewish Teachers opposed these truths, Math. 27.43. & 26.64. It was then the Devil in them, that knew him, who made them so speak, Mar. 1.34.

We may read in learned relations, of such, as in their fits,* would speak strange languages. *Fernelius*, an undoubted testimony, mentioned, how he saw an ignorant and frantic boy, and heard him in his madness to speak Greek. *Melanchton* says, that he saw a *Demoniac* woman in *Saxony*, who could neither write nor read, and yet spoke both Greek and Latin.

---

* Lib. de abd. verum causis, c. 16. Bodin. de Daeono. l. 3. c. 6.

VIII. When one divines, as the *Pythoness* did, Act. 16. & foretells to such as come to demand questions of things to come, or does reveal hidden things. As *Sleiden* in his Commentary tells of Anabaptistical Maids,[*] when some hid their monies, they would tell where they hid the same.

IX. When holy means is used, as Christ did by his Word and power, thē the party to cry with a loud voice, to before torn, & at the spirit's departing, to be left for dead in the judgment of the beholders, Mar. 1.26. & 9.26, Luk. 4 34 & 15.42. Thus it tell out with the possessed, recorded in holy Scriptures, Let the practices of Counterfeits be tried hereby, and also by the signs of those that are bewitched. Of which (in the next book and 12. Chapter) hereafter.

---

[*] *Anabaptists* are of the Christian faith who believe that the baptism of infants is meaningless since they do not decide for themselves to partake in the act. It is then only meaningful later in life when one decides to be cleansed from sin.

# CHAP. IV.

*That the Devil and evil spirits, through God's permission, may do much evil unto the godly for their trial, and unto the wicked for their punishment, without any association of Witches.*

IT is too common a received error, amongst the vulgars, yea, and amongst not a few persons of better capacity, that if any be vexed by a spirit, that such are bewitched. But it is a clear truth, that the Devil may afflict man or woman, their children and their cattle, without the knowledge, consent or association with any Witch.

1. The History of the Evangelists accuse the devil and unclean spirits, for all the vexations, torments, and tortures which many possessed endured, and not a word of any Witch, to set the Devil on work.

2. The people which brought the possessed to our Savior, complained only of the Devil, Matth. 15.22. Luk. 9.39. They made no mention of Witches, nor (for anything we read) had any suspicion of them.

3. We find that God has often sent the Devil, as the Executioner of his displeasure, without any means of a Witch, as amongst the Egyptians he sent evil angels, as before I have showed out of Psal. 78.49. between *Ahimelech* and the Sichemites, Judg. 9.23. So upon *Saul*, 1. Sam. 16.15. And so were a Legion sent by Christ into a Herd of Swine, Mar. 5 12. Thus we see Devils sent immediately from God, without any instigation of Witches, who are given over of God into the hands of the Devil: neither doth God use them, as his instruments to work by, as he doth by Devils, and other wicked men, in other cases: as he did by *Nebuchadnezzar* with his host, so by *Cyrus*, and others, to punish by them, whom he had determined so to deal with.

4. We read that the Devil entered into the Serpent, when there was yet no Witch, Gen. 3. He, when God gave him leave, entered into the Sabaeans, and Chaldeans to rob *Job* of his cattle. He burnt his sheep with fire, blew down the house upon all Job's children, and killed them, and at length tormented *Job's* body, and affrighted him with visions and dreams, Job 1. & 2. & 7.12. and without any setting on by a Witch.

5. The Scripture tells us, that Satan needs no provoker to set him forward: for the text says, that he compasses the world to and from, Job 1. and goes up and down like a roaring Lyon, seeking whom he may detour. 1. Pet. 5. He is ready, (if God give way) to be

a lying spirit in the mouths of *Ahab's* Prophets to seduce him, 1. King. 22. and to beguile them.[*]

6. Lastly, the Devil may take possession of a man or woman, not by the instigation of another, but this may come to pass by the very parties own default that is possessed, by invocating the Devil, as to say, *The Devil take me*, or, *Would the Devil had me*, if a thing be not so and so, which may be spoken in so unhappy a time, as God may give the Devil then leave to enter, of which there have been examples. 2. By intermeddling with curious Arts, and so become possessed of a Devil. 3. Or by buying a familiar spirit, [†] as a Gentleman did a Ring of another, wherein was, as he was told, a familiar enclosed, of whom he would know many things. Which Ring be at length (being displeased with the spirit for telling him many lies) one day cast into the fire, upon which the spirit seized upon him, and became his tormentor. A just plague to such as would confrere, hear and learn of a Devil. 4. Such as will increase their skill by Satan,[‡] as *Hermolans Barbarus* did, and as the Chymicke mekets, seeking the Philosopher's stone,

---

[*] See *for what sinnes the Diuell by Gods permission seizeth upon any. Delrio lib. 3. par. 1. quest. 7. sect. 2. p. 429.* pride, hatred, vncleannesse, persecuting the just, falling from truth, blasphemie, cursing, vnmercifulnes, & prophane contempt of holy things. See *the Theater of Gods iudgement in cursing*.

[†] *Bodin. de Demonomania.*

[‡] Cyted in *Roberts* his Treatise of Witchcraft, pag. 33.; *De Daemono.* l. 3. c. 3. p. 261.

but failing by their Art,* have asked counsel of the Devil, as *Bodinus* relates from an approved witness; it is just with God to let the Devil possess some of them.

Thus we see the Devil may be the sole Agent, without the fellowship of a Witch. And therefore this point the Gentlemen of the *Grand-Jury* are to take into their serious consideration: lest some be unjustly prosecuted and condemned, when the Devil only is the deed-doer, as they may see in the many instances before set down in holy Writ; and may be read in other Histories.

Also if such as be afflicted, or their friends, would consider with themselves, how that Satan may be the sole worker; it would

1. Make Atheistic hearts to shake off security, and work in them a dread & fear of God, when they shall consider a fiend of Hell, not sent of a Witch, but of God, to be their tormentor.

2. This would cause them to seek to God for help in the first place, knowing that he only, and none but he

---

* The philosopher's stone has been thought to be only discoverable through philosophy and the practice of alchemy. Although some believe the concept of the stone to be a symbol of philosophical understanding, a great many throughout history have believed it to be the discovery of a medicine or pill that could grant immortality, or the blueprint for the transmutation of metals into gold, both by way of alchemical discovery.

can overrule and command Satan, and make him to give over his practices.

3. If there be any grace in them, it will cause them to use holy means, such only as God allows of, as remedies to help them, as fasting and prayer, with a searching of their ways, and the reformation of their lives.

4. In this case they neither can tell how, nor dare to imagine which way to be revenged of the Devil, as the vain generation of men labor to be revenged upon suspected Witches, for sending the Devil; upon which Witches only they fly with violence, like raging tigers in heart, thinking so to remove a Devil from them, neglecting irreligiously the former sanctified means for their comfortable deliverance.

*But you will perhaps here ask, how one may know that Satan is the only Agent, without the consent of a Witch?

†I answer. 1. If there be not any suspicion at all of a Witch, but only some apparition of a spirit, as I could give herein a very rare instance of an afflicted person nearby me.

2. If there be a suspicion, yet the same not just, but an idle, vain, and foolish suspicion, without any good

---

* *Quest.*
† *Answ.*

ground, of which idle suspicions, you shall hear in the next Book.

3. If the suspicion be upon great probabilities, and very strong presumptions, yet unless these do lead to prove, that the suspected has made a league and compact with the Devils, he works not with them; but is the sole Agent: for without this league, he will not be an Agent for Witches. How to prove this league: see the second book, chap. 18.

4. If the suspected be proved a Witch, by making the league, yet for all this, it may be the Devil alone, except it can be proved, that the suspected Witch or Witches have procured Satan to afflict those, for whose cause they are prosecuted.

For although they be Witches, yet it will not therefore follow, that everyone afflicted in their bodies, or in their children, or in their servants, or in their cattle by Satan, are so vexed by the procurement of those Witches, except upon further proof, which must be inquired after; as the proof of their falling out, their malice in bitter cursing, their threats to be revenged of them, therefore telling of evils to befall them, the ill accidents which happen thereupon presently on a sudden, or in a very short time, of which more at large in the other Book, chap. 17.[*]

Thus by these may men discern, whether the Devil be the sole Agent or no. Before I end this Chapter,

---

[*] Book 2, chapter 17 of this volume.

some other Questions may be propounded touching Spirits or Devils.

Quest. 1. *What it is the Devil can do, if God be pleased to give him leave?*

*Answ.* To answer to this Question, I will take the Examples in holy Scripture; and so from thence gather the particulars.

*1. Gen. 3.1. Wee here learn, that the Devil may enter into a dumb creature. 2. That he can out of the same utter a voice intelligible. 3. That he will offer conference (if any will hearken to him) to deceive. 4. That he chooses the subtlest creature to deceive by, and the weaker vessel to confrere with. 5. He is powerful in his persuasions to overcome.

2. Exod. 7.11.22. and 8.7. with Psal. 78.49. He can deceive the eyesight, and seem to change one creature into another, as a Rod into a Serpent, Water into blood, and to make, as if Frogs were before us, and he can greatly trouble us.

3. Judg. 9 23. He can set people at odds, to deal treacherously one with another, and to make them rise up and murder one another, as this story shows.

4. 1. Sam. 16.14. He can trouble and terrify a man, and can also rap him beyond himself to make him

---

* See *Delrio de disq. mag. l. 2. q. 10.11.12.13.14. concerning the power of spirits.*

prophesy, chap. 18.10. as he did the Sybylles. He will force to murder, chap. 19.9.

5. Job 1. & 2. He can stir up wicked men to spoil and rob us, and to kill and murder our servants, chap. 1.15, 17. He can make fire fall down, as from heaven, to burn and consume man and beast, chap. 1.16. He can raise a wind to blow down our houses over our heads, and kill us, chap. 1.19. He can smite our bodies with sore Byles all over, chap. 2.7. He can scare us with dreams, and terrify us with visions, Job 7.14. & 6.4.

6. 1. Sam. 28.12, 14, 19. He can counterfeit the resemblance of a holy man, his person and his words, and relate truly things past,* and also foretell some things to come, as they shall fall out, as here, and as often has been found true, which he doth: 1. By his knowledge of divine prophecies, and his understanding of the drawing near of their accomplishment.† 2. By his exquisite skill in natural things, not only by the general causes, but the subordinate to them, with the particular operations, what necessarily they must produce. 3. By his diligent observation of innumerable instances, from the worlds beginning, of the periods of Kingdoms, and Families, of the causes of their changes, and ruin, and so conclude by experience of the like to come. 4. By his own, and his fellow Devils diligence in all places, whereby they are acquainted with all secret plots, consultations, resolutions, and preparations,

---

* How the Devil can tell things to come.
† *Delrio lib.* 4. *cap.* 1 *qu.* 1.2. *pag.* 529.

which they will relate to others, which know them not, as predictions, which are only that which they elsewhere see and hear. 5. By his own persuasions, and working through his suggestions in men's hearts, and his observing the effectual operations thereof, provoking to bring the same about, and so can foretell what such will do. Thus, he could have told of *Caine's* murdering of *Abel*, and of *Judas* his treason, because he had women them thereunto. 6. By his knowledge of God's will, to allow him to do this or that, as he did to Job, to *Abimelech* and the *Sichemites*, of which he could have foretold. Thus, can he tell many things, as he did Saul's death, and the *Israelites'* overthrow.

7. Matth. 4.3, 4. Here he dares to make an assault upon any, if thus upon our Savior. 2. He can take men and carry them from place to place. 3. He can set a glorious representation of these worldly things unto the eye. 4. He labors for a league, and to be worshipped.

8. Matth. 9.32. and 12.22. and 15.22. and 17.15. with Mark. 1.20. and 5.5, 7. and 7.26. and 9.17, 18.20, 22, 25, 26. and Luk. 4.35. and 7.2. and 8.29, 39. and 11.14. and 13.11, 16. Out of all which places we may observe, that the Devil can bereave one of his wits, and make one lunatic, deaf, dumb, and blind, bow the body together, so that one shall not be able to lift up himself. He can enter in, and possess any really, and make them invincibly strong, and work other effects: of all which, before in the latter part of the 3. chapter.

9. Acts 8.9, 10. and 16.16. He can be witch the people, making them believe, that his works are the great power of God: and can, by the tongue of the possessed, divine and foretell things, and utter great praises of the servants of God.

Quest. 2. *What sorts of persons may the Devil possess?*

*Answ.* Children, Luk. 13.6. Young folks, Mark. 7.26. Men, Mark. 5.2, 1, 23. Women, Luk. 13.16. Matth. 15.22. yea, such as be the elect of God. Job. Chap. 1. and 2. A daughter of Abraham, Luk. 13.11, 16, and Mary Magdalen, Luk. 7.2.

Quest. 3. *How long may people be thus vexed by Satan?*

*Answ.* For a long time, Luk. 8.27. from a child, till one be grown up, Mar. 9.21. even 18. years Luke. 13.16.

Quest. 4. *How many Devils may be in one at once?*

*Answ.* Seven, Luk. 7.2, and more, Luk. 11.26. yea a whole legion, Mark. 5.9.

Quest. 5. *May not a Devil and a good Angel be together in one man?*

*Answ.* I think not; for of good Angels I read, that they pitch about the godly, Psal. 34. they guide and bear up the godly in their ways, Psal. 91. and are

ministering Spirits, sent forth to minister for them
that be heirs of salvation, Heb. 1.14. but of entering
into them, I read not.

Again, that a Devil may be *ventriloquists*, I have
heard, and read of, but never of a good Angel to be
so.

Moreover, for him to be in a godly man, there is no
necessity, to plead for him against a Devil; he having
the holy Spirit, and by him the Word of God, for
instruction and comfort. And to conceit him to be in
an unclean person, a vain and loose liver, and one of
an unreformed life, * sensual, void of the Spirit of
grace, to comfort him, is beyond all warrant of holy
Scripture.

Object. But it will be said, *that two have been heard
some times to speak in one man, one like a Devil, in
a great voice, and another pleading against him with
a small voice.*

*Answ.* What then? 1. May not one Devil counterfeit
two voices, as well as one man can, very artificially,
three or four, one after another? If they speak at once
together, there is two; but it cannot be concluded, that
there are two, because of the change of voice, and
one speaking after another.

Secondly, If two be supposed, they may be both
Devils, for all their pleading, as is recorded in a book

---

* Jude. 19.

entitled, *The admirable history of a Magician*, where, in one person was a Dialogue between *Verrin* a little Devil, who spoke all after a holy manner, and *Beelzebub* the great Devil, who spoke wickedly, and blasphemously. The one counterfeiting the possessed, the other, threatening and terrifying. The pretended good Angell, is the worse Devil, soothing up the vain man in a foolish conceit of God's great favor, as having an Angell sent for his souls safeguard, as if he were so precious in God's eyes, to witness him to be his by an Angel, to whom the Lord has not vouchsafed his Spirit to witness his Adoption, in the work of Regeneration. A very illusion.

Quest. 6. *When the Devil is in one, how he may be cast out?*

*Answ.* 1. Not by any power in, or of man: for Satan is the strong Man, in Matth. 12.29. Mark. 3.27. whom man cannot bind, or overmaster.

2. Not by any force of Popish Exorcisms, as Romish* Priests brag: for wee read of Priests, yea chief Priests, professed Exorcists, adjuring spirits in the name of Jesus, and yet the *Demoniac* set upon them and wounded them. † Moreover we may read, how Romish Exorcists have used their Exorcisms, above a year together, upon one person, and never the

---

* The old equivalent of Roman.

† Io. Bap. Romilian a superiour.

better.* *Bodinus*,† in his *Daemonomania*, tells us of a Devil, that told them, that he would not come out for any man's sake, but for a Priest called Motanus who was a Magician. So little cares the Devil for a Priests power in Exorcising.‡ Their words cannot conjure a Devil: for if they could work effectually, what need they set up so many Counterfeits, to pretend to be possessed, on whom they might show their imagined power? To which, if any Devil has at any time yielded, it was because he would, and not for that he was enforced thereunto, to beguile the superstitious Exorcists and others, relying upon such means.

3. Not by the power of any great Devil, to force out another, as our Savior teaches, Matth. 12.25, 26. Mar. 3.23, 24. And therefore not by Art Magick, which believers do detest, Act. 19.19. as being the Devil's intention, to which he may voluntarily yield, to uphold the devilish Art; but by which he cannot be forced, because both the Art and the practice is from his own self.

---

* Exorcisms have been recorded throughout history and early protestants believed that the Roman Catholics use rites and rituals similar to that of necromancy. Since Jesus was able to cast out demons with one command, the use of length rituals and incantations was thought to be meaningless.

† Io. Billet in the admirable History of a Magician.

‡ See the B. called the *boy of Bilson*, against the Romish Exorcists.

Therefore devils are to be cast out only by the finger of God, Luk. 11.20. even by the power of his holy Spirit, Matth. 12.28.

And the means to have this aide of the power of God, is to be obtained by fasting and prayer, Math. 17.21. Mar. 9.29. And this was the only means in the Primitive Church, & not by Exorcisms, [*] as even *Bodinus* a Papist does witness, and cited the testimony of *Austin, Chrysostom, Clement, Sozomenus*, and the practices of Saint *Hilarion*, who without the host, without adjuration, without questioning with the Devil, by only using prayer to God, cast out the Devil. In ancient times the *Daemoniacs*, says the same Author, were brought into the Congregation, and their public prayers were made to cast out the Devil, and such means have prevailed in these our days, and warrant we have from Christ and his ancient Church to use the same, and not these superstitious, idolatrous, and very diabolical practices of the Romish Antichristians.

Quest. 7. *Whether the Devils be willing to depart easily out of the possessed?*

*Answ.* No verily; as appeared from the plain evidence of the Scripture, by their crying, when they were to come out. Act. 8.7. By tearing the possessed, when they were commanded to come out, Luk. 15. 42. and 4 35. By their petitioning Christ to send them into other creatures; as swine, before they would go out,

---

[*] Lib. 3. c. 6. *de Demonomania*

Matth. 8. 31. By the force of the Word, which says, that they were cast out. By that place of Luke 9.39. which sees, that he hardly departed. Lastly, by the Devils acknowledging it to be a torment, to be commanded to come out of the man, Luk. 8.28, 29.

If then there be no forcing of him, but by the power of God, through fasting and prayer performed in faith: but that the Devil goes out, and leaves the afflicted willingly: great cause there is to suspect (if there be no counterfeiting) that the Devil does, one way or other, some greater mischief, or else intends to return again, with seven other worse than himself, and so make the last state of the party worse than the first, Mat. 12.45.

# CHAP. V.

*That seeing men, or women, or beasts may be afflicted, from some natural causes: or that some persons may counterfeit cunningly many things: or that the Devil may be the sole worker, without consent of a Witch: people are not rashly and in the first place to ascribe the cause to witchcraft.*

IT is an evil too common amongst the ignorant vulgars, amongst the superstitious, the popishly-affected, amongst others of a vain conversation, which are Protestants at large, neutrals in heart, sensual, without the power of Religion, and amongst all the generation of vain people, to think presently, when any evil betides them, that they, or theirs, or their cattle are bewitched, that some man or woman has brought this evil upon them. From which irreligious & uncharitable thought, so prejudicial to their soul's safety, many reasons may withdraw them.

I. The consideration of God's own hand, of some natural causes, of some power of Satan, without any Witch, as in the former Chapter is showed at large.

II. An approved truth by long experience, that such as little dream of Witches, and lightly regard them, are hardly at any time or never troubled with them: but on the contrary, such as ever live in suspicion of them, such as fear them, give to them for fear, and upon any ill hap are ever dreaming, that they are the instruments, and are most plagued by them, which plainly shows, that this their suspicion, fear, and ascribing their harms to Witches, do much displease God, who makes them to feel the smart thereof.

III. All do grant, which have any knowledge of the power of Witches, that they work by the Devil; they curse, ban, threaten: but he works the mischief. Therefore keep off the Devil, and there is no fear of a Witch. She may bid him go, but that is, if he himself lift; or if he please, to satisfy her revengeful heart, he must have leave from God. For her sending gives not, nor increases any power in the Devil, either to work his own, or her malice upon any. If a man's own sins provoke not God, if our ways please him, and that he hedge us about (Job 1.) we need fear neither Witch, nor Devil. But let us cease to sin, fear God, obey him, and we shall be safe enough.

IV. The manifold evils which happen and fall out upon this so present imaginary conceit to be bewitched.

1. It withdraws men's minds from the consideration of God's hand so, as they do not humble themselves before him, as they ought.

2. It makes them think, that though it be a Devil that afflicts them, yet that he neither is sent of God (as ill spirits sometimes be) nor that he comes of his own malicious disposition against mankind (when the Scriptures show the contrary) but that the Witch only has sent him, else had he not come to torment them. So as here their thoughts are wholly upon the Witch, as if he or she were the only commander and ruler in this action.

3. The Devil hereupon takes great advantage, and works mightily upon such persons, which be so apt to believe themselves to be bewitched: For

First, he works in them a slavish fear, to stand more in awe of the creature, then of the Creator.

Secondly, upon this fear, if anything happens amiss, he suggested a suspicion of this or that party to be a Witch.

Thirdly, the suspicion a little settled, he then stirs the man or woman to utter the suspicion of this or that neighbor.

Fourthly, the Devil works credulity in those neighbors, and withal sets them on work to second the relation, with opening of their suspicious thoughts of the same party; and withal, to tell what they have either heard from others, or observed from themselves, that may tend to increase the suspicion, that such an one is a Witch.

Fifthly, through this credulity, this relation, and rumoring this suspicion, from one rattling Gossip to another, it is taken for granted, that such a one is a Witch, and has bewitched such a man, woman, child, servant, or beast.

Sixthly, upon this grows a general dislike, with a fear of the said party suspected, so as others upon any ill hap, begin likewise to blame the same party for that ill accident.

Seventhly, to make up the Devil's plotted mischief herein; he makes the party suspicious to mark all the words and deeds of the suspected, and to interpret the worst of them, to gather matter to accuse the same of Witchcraft. And to perform this, the Devil persuades some to seek to a Wizard for help and counsel, which hell-hound tells them, that they are bewitched, that they live by ill neighbors: and hereupon returning home, they publish it amongst their neighbors, that now without all peradventure, such an one is indeed a Witch, and has done this and that harm.

Lastly, hereupon the Devil stirs up some more impatient, more fiery and enraged thē the rest, to seek revenge, to hale the suspected before Authority, to procure his or her imprisonment, and at last, perhaps, follow him or her to death, which is that which in all these things the Devil labored for. For he is a murderer, and delights in blood-shedding, especially of innocent blood, as it may fall out in this case, and (as learned men write) sometimes it doth, upon only fallible presumptions.

V. And lastly, they may be drawn from this their rash conceit so sudden, and soon in their mind, by the Scriptures silence, nowhere ascribing tortures, pains, vexations, anguish in mind or body, losses of cattle or other goods to Witches; but to *God's hand*, Job 1.21. Psal. 39.9. or to *men* openly and violently wronging, robbing, spoiling and killing, as in Job 1.15, 17. or to Devils, Matth. 15.22. Luk. 9.39. but, as is said, nowhere in all the Bible to Witches.

Quest. *It may here be demanded, why the Scriptures do not anywhere ascribe, (as men do now) bodily harms unto Witches, seeing there is such mention of Witches and Witchcraft in many places?*

*Ans.* The Scriptures of God do never assign instruments to be set on work by him, which have not power in themselves to do what he employs them about, whether it be Angell, Devil, Man, or any other creature; nor ascribes unto them any deed, which they cannot do of themselves, without the help of some other: But Witches are Satan's slaves, who cannot do those evils, which men accuse them of, but the Devil does it for them. Therefore, the Scriptures ascribe the Acts to the Devil as his own, and not unto Witches (though they consent) because they do them not themselves.

II. It is done in special wisdom from God, to teach all that be godly (for whose sakes the Scriptures are penned, and who indeed make them their rule and guide) to ascribe least unto Witches, or rather nothing at all in this kind to them, as the multitude do. But to judge of a Witch as a Witch, and of her actions, as they are in the practices of Witchcraft, distinct from the working of the Devil, and her or his consent with the Devil in evils. For so shall Witchcraft be detested as Witchcraft, as it ought to be; and not only because of the mischiefs which befall men thereby, as generally men imagine, which yet are the Devils', and not the Witches' practices, as shall in the book following be more fully declared.

# A GUIDE TO

# GRANDJURY MEN.

# ~ The second Book. ~

## CHAP. I.

### *That there are Witches.*

Though some have gone about to prove that there are no Witches: yet the contrary tenant is undeniably true, that there are Witches.

1. From the laws that God himself has made against them: 1. Forbidding the practice of Witchcraft, and that none amongst his should be Witches, Wizards, Necromancers, and such like, Deut. 18.10, 11, 12. 2. Forbidding any to go to them, Levit. 19. & 20. Isa. 8.19. 3. His commandment to put Witches to death, Exod. 22.18. If there were no Witches, what need these laws?

II. From the History of the Bible, which names to us certain Witches, as the Sorcerers of Egypt, Exo. 7.

*Iannes* and *Iambres*, 2. Tim. 3 8. Those in Babylon, and Persia, Dan. 2. & 5.7. Isa. 47.12. Those amongst the Philistines, Isa. 26. and among the Nations driven out before the Israelites, Deut. 18. 12, 13. So we read of other Witches which were of *Balaam*, Numb. 22. Jos. 13.22. of *Iezabel*, 2. King. 9.22. of *Manasses*, 2. Chron. 33.6. of *Simon Magus*, Act. 8.9. and *Elymas*, Act. 13.1, 2. It makes mention of the practices of Witches. Exod. 7.2. Chr. 33. 6. Isa. 47.9. Ezek. 21.21 Hest. 3.7. Thirdly, it speaks of some going to them, 1. Sam. 28.7. and sending to them, Num. 22.5. Jos. 24.9. Fourthly, It relates how some Kings put them to death. 1. Sam. 28.3, 9. and cut them off, 2. King. 23.24. All this should be false, if there were no Witches.

III. From comparisons and similies fetched from Witchcraft by *Samuel*, 1. Sam. 15. & by Isa. 29.4. which were absurd, if there were no such thing.

IV. From Saint *Paul's* mentioning Witchcraft amongst the works of the flesh, Gal. 5.20.

V. From God's threatening damnation upon Sorcerers, Reu. 21.8.

VI. Experience of the truth, both amongst ourselves and in other Countries.

VII. The confession of infinite number of Witches condemned and executed.

VIII. The truth of Histories and many relations of their arraignments, and conviction.

IX. The laws of nations both Heathen and Christian against them. It is idle to spend time farther in so manifest a truth, therefore hereof, thus much briefly.

# CHAP. II.

## *What kind & sorts of persons they be, which are most apt to become Witches.*

Witchcraft being, as S. *Paul* says, amongst the fruits of the flesh, Gal. 5. 20. one may fall into this sin, as well as into any other, if God prevent it not.

And albeit there be men Witches, as *Balaam*, and *Elymas*; and women Witches, as the Witch of *Endor*; and of both these sexes, of all sorts, young, middle and old age; of all which, instances may be given: yet of Witches there be commonly more women than men: this is evident,

I. From God's publishing his Law against Witches, Exo. 22.18. in the feminine gender. *Praestigiatricem ne sinito viuere.*\*

II. From Saul's speech, when he said, Seek me out a woman that has a *Familiar spirit*, 1. Sam. 28.7. 1. Chr. 10.13, 14. In naming a woman, and not a man,

---

\* Do not allow a sorceress to live.

it seems that women were more addicted to this than men.

III. From experience it is found true here, and in all countries, especially of hurting Witches.

IV. From Stories, and relations, even from these in our own Kingdom: as of the Witches in *Lancashire*; in one of their meetings, there were of nineteen or twenty assembled, but two or three men. The Witches bewitching, the Earle of Rutland's children, were women. Those *Warby* were women, and but one man. Women exceed the men, and it may be for these reasons.

1. Satan his setting upon these rather than on men, since his unhappy onset and prevailing with *Eve*.

2. Their more credulous nature, and apt to be misled and deceived.

3. For that they are commonly impatient, and more superstitious, and being displeased, more malicious, and so more apt to bitter cursing, and far more revengeful, according to their power, then men, and so herein more fit instruments of the Devil.

4. They are more tongue-ripe, and less able to hide what they know from others, and therefore in this respect, are more ready to be teachers of Witchcraft to others, and to leave it to children, servants, or to some others, then men.

5. And lastly, because where they think they can command, they are more proud in their rule, and more busy in setting such on work whom they may command, then men. And therefore, the Devil labors most to make them Witches: because they, upon every light displeasure, will set him on work, which is that which he desires. See instances in Bodin, in his *Daemonomania*. l. 2. cap. 3. p. 144. 150. and the Confession of Mother *Demdike* a *Lancashire* Witch: for he will ask and press to be commanded: and if he be called upon, and not set on work, it may cost the party his or her life: so displeased is he, if he be not set on work, which women will be ready enough to do.

But whether they be men, or women, these sorts following are the aptest to be the Devils Scholars herein.

I pass by the Infidels, Heathen people in former ages (from whom these abominations mentioned in Deut. 18.9, 10, 11. came into Israel) as also Pagans, and salvage Nations now, (amongst whom, by Travelers relations, Witchcraft is rise) and I will speak only of such sorts as be called Christians, and these be

The *sottish ignorant*, whose eyes are blinded by Satan, 2. Cor. 4.4. and are led captive by him, 2. Cor. 2.26. This appeared in those Witches, which commonly are detected amongst us, ignorant, silly sottish persons, most of them.

The *malicious spirits*, *impatient people*, *and full of revenge*, having hearts swollen with rancor, upon the least displeasure, being bitter banners, and cursers, and threatening requital. This is manifest, by the nature, quality, words and deeds of Witches convicted, who have showed themselves to be such, and ever found to be so. To these may be added,

Astrologians, * monthly Prognosticators, Diviners, Figure casters, Fortune-tellers, Charmers, Observers of times, of lucky and unlucky days: for all these are reckoned up, where Witches, Wizards, Enchanters, and Sorcerers are forbidden, Deut. 18. 10, 11. Isa. 47.12, 13.

†Jugglers also and such legerdemain‡ companions, who strive to deceive the eyes, and withal use speeches, as if they dealt with a familiar, saying, *Hey Jack, up aloft, Jack, Pass, and repass, Jack, for thy Master's advantage*. Though they thus speak, to beguile people, and sometimes with a *Mole's* skin stuffed, or a *Rat's*, by candle-light in a corner, fear simple fools, doing that they do by activity and nimbleness of the hand. Yet for that they sport with such resemblances, and utter words, as the invocating of a spirit: the reality whereof is called abomination before God, it may be just with God, to give over such, (by Law, Rogues) into Satan's snares and deceits, to make them his own in earnest, whose

---

* Of Astrol. See *Delrio*. l. 4. c. 3.4.1.

† Of Jugglers and their tricks, See *Scot.* B. 13. *cap*. 23.24. 34.

‡ Slight of Hand

they would seem to be in sport, being lewd and vain fellows, children of disobedience, as Saint *Paul* speaks. To these add Tumblers, Gypsies, Rogues, and such like, apt to be made Satan's slaves in Witchery, as they be otherwise his in impiety.

Such as profess to cure diseases, but by such means, as have no reason in the work of nature to do the cure, not has by any ordinance of God from his Word any such operation to heal the infirmity, and therefore such remedies must be diabolical, and the practitioners either Witches already, by their implicit faith, or the next door to Witches: such be they, as use Spells, Charms, and which cure a wound by anointing the instrument which made it, and such like.

To these may be added, such as D. *Cotta* a Physician reckons up in a discourse of his, Empericks, Quacksalvers, Ephemerides masters, wandering Chirurgions, and such like.

Those that are given to curiosity, to seek after vain knowledge, in pride of heart to go beyond others, to understand secrets, & hidden things, to know things to come. Such as these, not bounding themselves within the limits of reason, nor of God's revealed will, fall foul at unawares upon the Devil, and are in great danger to be entrapped by him, and by his enticements made his slaves. Thus was *Faustus* taken,* so some *Alchymisters*† caught, seeking for the Philosophers stone.

For curiosity of knowledge, if Reason and Art fail, will moue men to seek help of a spirit, who is ready at hand attending their call, and to draw them into this pit of Magick, Sorcery and Witchcraft. A just plague for proud & profane wits. Of this danger speaks one Master *Cooper*:‡ from which he and another by God's preventing grace, was delivered.

Those that with insatiable greediness gape after worldly wealth, and immeasurably thirst after Honors, as did *Sylvester* the 2. *Benedict* 8. *Alexander* 6. Joh. 20. & 21. who gave themselves to Magick and Witchcraft,§ and so to the Devil, to come to be Popes.

Those that be superstitious and idolatrous, as all Papists be. That of these very many the Devil works upon to make Witches, is not to be doubted: for Sorcery is the practice of that Whore, the Romish Synagogue, Revel. 18.23. Secondly, it is found true, that healing Witches do use many of their superstitious Ceremonies, Lip-prayers, Ave-Marys,** Creeds, and Pater-nosters by set numbers. Thirdly, when Popery bear sway here, then Devils and Spirits often appeared, and at that time were

---

* Bodiu. *de Daemo*. l. 3. cap. 3. *Detrio* lib. 6, *monit.* 7, 8. pag. 1048, 1049.

† Alchemists

‡ Mystery of Witchcraft, pag. 12.

§ See the Pageant of Popes and Benne.

** Hail Mary prayers

many more Witches then now. Fourthly, they allow of Conjurers and diabolical Exorcisms. Witchery tricks, intentions of Satan. * Fifthly, where that Jewish, heathenish, and heretical religion is, there still are innumerable Witches.† *Bodin* relates, that one *Trescalanus* a notorious Witch, in *Charles* the 9. days, having his life given to discover others, told the King that there were in his Kingdom above 300,000. Also the same *Bodinus*; tells us, that there had been executed in Loraine, while one man *Remingius* was Governor there, nine hundred Witches. Sixthly, and lastly, we may read in the Ad*mirable History of a Magician*, set out by Papists, and dedicated to the Q. Regent of France, that the Devil called *Verrine*, justified most of the superstitious and idolatrous practices in that Church, as Transubstantiation, *Worshiping the Host, Invocation of Saints and Angels*, with the rest: Is it not likely then, that there the Devil can have power over the Professors of that Religion, which he so well likes, and approves of? This is evident in this something, that so many Priests, Religious men, and religious women of their orders, have been found to be Witches, as Bodinus has less recorded to posterities in his *Daemonomania*. Thus, we see the sorts, which principally may be ensnared by Satan, to turn Witches.

---

* See the Boy of Bilson.
† *De Daemon*. lib. 4. cap. 5.

# CHAP. III.

*Before the Devil come to solicit to Witchcraft,*
*he sends some preparedness in such parties,*
*to give him hope to prevail.*

The miserable man or woman which becomes a
Witch, makes way for the Devil to set upon them, to
make them such. He goes thither, where he is either
sure, or well hopes of entertainment, Mat. 12.44, 48.
He therefore watches the time when he may best
offer his service unto them.

The preparedness (besides that which is common, as
impenitency, profaneness, unconscionableness, and
irrespective to the power of Religion) are
distempered passions, and violence of affections,
vain curiosities, I company, through which occasions
he taketh advantage, and works to have his will. As
for example:

When any fall into a *passionate sorrow*, *
accompanied with solitariness, for some loss, as did
a woman for the death of her child: in which
sorrowful melancholy mood, the Devil offered
himself to comfort her. So at that time to others a lso
in the time of a great death, extremely pinched, and

---

* In a discourse of Spirits, by *Sebastian Michaelis* D. of Divinity.
a Friar.

in desperate cases, he appeared, and at length won the former woman, and these to become Witches: for which they were afterwards (being found out, confessing how they so became such) condemned, and executed.

When a man is impatient of poverty, and will needs be rich, even against Gods providence, here is preparation for a Devil.[*] As we may read of a young man thus affected, to whom the Devil offered himself to supply his wants, and to fulfill his desire, if he would become his; to which he yielded, and wrote a band with his own blood for the ratification.

[†]When one is enraged with anger, plotting revenge, here is work for the Devil: Thus he took hold of one *Mary Smith* of *Lynne*, and brought her to be a Witch, and to make a league with him.

[‡]When one is familiar with such as are Witches: Thus one *Alice Nutter*, a rich woman in *Lancashire* was seduced, and one *Alison Deuice*, and *Anne Chattox*, which they confessed, and were executed for their murders and Witchcrafts.

When any are addicted to the reading and study of dangerous books, enticing to the practice of hidden Mysteries of Magick, and Enchantments. Thus was *Lewis Gaufredy*,[§] a Priest, caught, and became a

---

[*] Fox in Acts and Monuments. sol. 789. last edition.
[†] Master Roberts treatise of VVitchcraft, p2, 46.
[‡] Tryall of Witchcraft in *Lancaster*.
[§] See the book of the life & death of *Lewis Gaufredy*.

Witch, a very Devil incarnate, in the height of villainies for his pride and treacheries.

Thus by these, and other like means, which may be gathered from the confessions of Witches, they prepare themselves for Satan's temptations to draw them to Witchcraft.

# CHAP. IV.

## Of Satan's appearing in some visible shape, to those that he entices to Witchcraft.

When the Devil has once perceived a man or woman's preparedness,[*] he taketh his sit time to discover himself, in some visible form to be seen of them.

That he can take a shape, it's not to be doubted; For,

1. He appeared in a form like *Samuel* to *Saul*, 1. Sam. 28. And Diviners do think, that the servants that came so immediately one upon another, to bring Job heavy tidings, were Devils, Job I. and it is held, that he appeared to Christ visibly, Matth. 4.

[†]2. Histories make mention of his visible appearing, and such as do write *de spectris, de bonis & malis Angelis*,[‡] affirm as much.

3. Witches generally confess it, as we may read in the relations of those many in Lancashire, those in

---

[*] *Delrio, lib.* 2. q. 27 *Sect* 1. of Satan's visible appearance.
[†] *Zanch. de op. lib.* 6. *die.* l. 4. *cap.* 16.
[‡] The specters of the good and bad Angels.

Northampton and Bedfordshire, and in all other places.

Now these appear not in one, but in variety of shapes and forms, as in the shape of a Man, or Woman, or a Boy, of a brown and white Dog, of a Foal, of a spotted Bitch, of a Hare, Mole, Cat, Kitling, Rat, dune Chicken or Owl, of a Toad, or Crab; of these have I read in the narrations of Witches, to which more may be added; for no doubt he can, if God permit, take any form upon him, for his advantage to deceive; though some write, that he cannot take the form of a Dove, or Lamb.[*]

We may in reading find, that he varies in his appearances, according to the nature, quality and condition of the persons to whom he presents himself. To base, for did, filthy, nasty and blockish, more beastlike then Christian people, he comes in the baser forms and more abhorred shapes: to some of them in the shape of Toads, as you have heard, to be loathed, even of nature itself, if they had not lost it. But to a Faustus, in a religious persons habit, to Gaufredy a Priest, one of some learning and wealth, he appears in some human shape, like a gallant fellow, and so unto others: for he fashions himself so, as he knows to be best liked, to whom he comes to show himself, to make them his.

---

[*] *Delrio, lib*. 2. q. 28 *Sect*.3.

# CHAP. V.

### *Of the league between the Devil and the Witch, with the sealing and confirmation.*

When the Devil has once appeared unto them, he leaves them not, till he get them to make an express league with him.[*]

This he procures of some, sometimes at the first coming, sometimes of others, not before the second, or third coming; for all yield not so readily to this alike: but howsoever; he is so importunate for this, that he at length prevails withal to make them yield.

The league on the man or woman's part is,[†] to give their souls to him (which he most commonly asks, as Witches have confessed) and to renounce God, as has been also acknowledged by Gaufredy and others: sometimes the Devil asks not only the soul (as he asks it of the sottish sort, which care not for it, so they may think their bodies safe) but he also asks the whole person, and sometimes his goods spiritual and temporal, as the Devil dealt with Gaufredy,[‡] as he plainly confessed before he was burnt, who gave himself body and soul, and all to Lucifer. The

---

[*] See the testimony of many, in *Detrio lib*. 5. *Sect*. 16. *pag*. 659. l. 2. q. 4. pa 99.

[†] In *Lavesshire*, *Bodin*. l. 2. cap. 4.

[‡] In *Lavesshire*, *Bodin*. l. 2. *cap*. 4.

Covenant on the Devil's part, is his promise, to help the poor to food, the sick to health, the ireful to be revenged, the curious to knowledge, the ambitious to honor, as he did the forenamed Popes, and the satisfying of lust to the lecherous, as he did to Gaufredy, to whom the devil gave a seedule[*] signed by himself, comprehending the virtue and power of his breath, to inflame any woman or maid with lust, if he could but breathe on them.

This league is uttered either by word of mouth, of such as cannot write; or in writing by others, and that by their own blood: so did Faustus also the young men spoken of by Master Fox: so have others done (as Bodin relates) and have subscribed the band with their own hands;[†] thus many have confessed. And Bodinus delivers it for a most certain truth, that such as exercise the Art of Witchcraft, of what kind so ever (if the Devil have visibly appeared) do make an express league with Satan.

This league being thus made and sealed, he has a sacrifice offered unto him of some, & of others some (as of their ordinary Witches) he desires to suck blood: for he will have his Covenant sealed with blood one way or other.

He sucks in divers parts of the body, as on the crown of the head,[‡] as the boys of Bradley, on the breasts

---

[*] In his life and death.

[†] *Lib* 2. *cap*. 4. in Confut. Wieri.

[‡] Lancashire Witch.

under the paps, as Alison Deuices, on the thighs,[*] as Mother Suttons and Mary her daughters, under the right ear,[†] as Joane Willimots: under the left flank, as Hellen Greenes: the neck, as Philip Flowers: in the secret parts, as Margaret Flowers: the chin, as Mother Samuels of Warboys.[‡] Thus the devils choose their sucking places, as they please; which they do, as some have confessed at the change,[§] or full of the Moon, or when they are set on work by the Witches.

Besides this sucking, they leave marks upon them, sometimes like a blue spot, as it was on Alizon Deuice, or like a little teat, as it was on Mother Sutton and her daughter, of Milton Milles in Bedfordshire.

These marks are not only, nor always in the sucking place, for the mark was not on Mother Samuels chin of Warboys, but they be often in other very hidden places, as under the eye-brows, within the lips, under arm-pits, on the right shoulders, thigh, flank, in the secret parts,[**] and seat.

Now after all these assurances made between them, that Satan may claim them for his own, then comes he to be familiar with them. All have not one familiar spirit, but some have more than others. Some indeed have but one, as old Denob dike: some have two, as

---

[*] In Bedfordshire.

[†] In Lancashire.

[‡] Warboy Witch.

[§] Hellen Greenes.

[**] Bodin. *de Damon*. l. 2. *cap*. 4.

Chattox, Joane Flower,* & Willimot: some three, as one Arthur Bill: some nine, as Mother Samuels of Warboys.

To these they give names; such as I have read of are these: *Mephastophilus,* † *Lucifer,* ‡ *Little Lord, Fimodes, David, Inde, Little Robin, Smacke, Lightfoot, Non-such, Lunch, Makeshift, Swart, Pluck, Blue, Catch, White, Callico, Hard name, Tibb, Hiff, Ball, Puss, Rutterkin, Dick, Prettie, Griffet* and *Jack.* And they meet together to Christen the spirits (as they speak) when they give the spirit a name.

By these familiar spirits they do what they do; these they ask counsel of, they send abroad to effect their desires, if God give leave, and they do verily think, that they have these spirits at command, upon the making of this damnable and most abominable league, to do whatsoever they please to serthem about.

---

* Witches in Northampton shire.

† Also, Mephistopheles. In the epic poem of Faust written by Goeth, Faust makes a compact with this demon.

‡ Warboys Witch. Leicestershire. Lancashire Witches. In *Gifford* Diall. of Witchcraft.

# CHAP. VI.

*That such an express league is made with the Devil:*
*why he entices his unto it, and how it is possible,*
*that any Christian should so be overtaken,*
*to yield thereunto.*[*]

Though some may question the truth of this compact, as if such a thing could be gained at any man's hands that knows what a Devil is, even man's mortal and irreconcilable enemy, yet is this a certain truth.

1. From variety of Scripture, in Psal. 58.5. the words are to be read thus; The mutterer joining societies cunningly: that is, the Witch with spirits.

2. From the Hebrew word, *Chabor*, an Enchanter, Deut. 18.11. Isa. 47.9, 12. which signifies one joined to another in league and society.

Now what other can that be, with whom the Enchanter is in league, but the Devil?

---

[*] Deliro. l. 5. Sect. 16. p. 659.

3. From the confession of Witches generally. *
Cyprian (whether the ancient Father or no, I am not
certain; for some affirm, some question it)
confidently from his own knowledge avers is, that all
make the league, as he once did, when he practiced
art Magick. The story of Faustus confirmed it, and all
the relations of Witches with us, as before is noted in
the other Chapter.

4. And lastly, the marks found upon Witches, and
also the bloody bonds sometimes, do strengthen the
truth of this.† For the young man's bond, of whom
Master Fox speaks, was thrown into the Assembly,
gathered together in prayer for his delivery from
Satan.

Quest. If any ark why Satan so labors for this
Covenant?

‡I answer, It may be, I. To anger the Lord in imitating
him, (as he labors to do in all things) but yet therein
to oppose him: for as God makes a Covenant with his,
so will the devil with his: as God has his seat of his
Covenant, so will the devil have his marks as God
confirms his by blood, so will the Devil have blood
to ratify the Covenant, which he and his make.

---

* Confession De duplici Martyrie. (Confession of a double
martyrdom)
† The mark, also known as the *bloody bond*.
‡ *Answ.* See *for Satan's imitation of God*, the last Chapter in this
Book.

2. To increase the sin of the Witches, to make them desperately wicked without hope of mercy, when they shall remember how they have renounced God, and given themselves to the devil, and thereby have provoke the just wrath of God to their utter damnation, which is that which Satan herein labors for.

3. To make them hereby surely his own, without starting back, if possibly it may be.

4. To beguile them the more cunningly, when hereby he makes them believe, that as they are his, so now he is theirs, at every call to be commanded, and to do what they would have him to do, according to their lusts.

This conceit pleases them greatly, by this they grow proud in heart, that they have spirits at command to tell them things, to teach them cures, to revenge their wrong, to work fear of themselves in others, to have in many things their wills and desires; by these are they so fast tied, as they always hold on this hellish trade, even to death, except the Lord prevent some with his more special grace.

If any wonder how it may be possible, that any reasonable soul, endued with any knowledge of God, and of the nature of a Devil, should thus be enthralled, let him weigh these things:

1. That man has lost the image of God, in which he was created, and is wholly polluted with sin and corruption.

*2. That hereby he is become of very near kin unto the Devil, even his own babe.

†3. That being his child, he will do his father's lusts, and that, no doubt, in one thing as well as in another; for men love darkness more than the light;‡ yea and naturally are given to work all uncleanness, even with greediness, so captivated are they to their lusts.

4. That man given over to his unruly passions, is violent, inconsiderate, and vehemently greedy to have his desired ends, by what means so-ever he can attain them; which makes him seek means of the Devil, to become enjoyer of his inordinate desires, regarding more the having of his present will, then respecting his future state after death: and is more taken up to obtain what he likes for the body and outward estate in the world, then with care of his spiritual condition and estate before God, which the natural man very little, or nothing at all regards.

5. That Satan has his wills, Ephes. 11. his devices. 2. Cor. 2. 11. his depth and policies, Rev. 2.24. his snares to catch people at unawares, 1. Tim. 3.7. 2. Tim. 2.26.

---

* 1. Job. 3.10.

† John. 8.44.

‡ John 3.19. Ephes. 4.19.

6. That hereupon he being thus furnished, he dare set upon any; yea, even upon Christ himself, to felicity him, yea, and that to a most execrable impiety, even to have Christ to fall down and to worship him a Devil; * for he watches opportunities, he seeks occasions, and the least offered, he espies, and quickly taketh the same, and so prevails often, not only with the rude and sottish, but with the greatest spirits, and sharpest wits sometimes.

7. That he has over mere natural men a ruling power, Ephes. 2.2. who are already in his snare, and at his own will are taken captive, 2. Tim. 2.26.

8. And lastly, that being given over of God unto Satan's temptation in this kind, how can they resist? Man is weak, Satan is strong, and withal subtle to beguile, they may easily therefore yield. All these things now considered, it is no wonder to know man to be thus seduced, and thus by this league to apostate so from God.

* Matth. 4.

# CHAP. VII.

## *That besides the former expressed league, there is a secret league made with Satan by some, and who they be.*

IT is a general tenant of Divines, which write of this subject, that there is a double league, the one open and expressly made with the Devil visibly appearing, of which in the former Chapter: the other is close, secret, and implicit, in a mutual consent, but without any express terms from either the one or the other, as in the former.

With this league the Devil contents himself sometimes, to wit, there, where he will perceives that the party will not be brought unto the other, which is such a one, as he intends not to employ, otherwise then about seeming good things: or such an one, as he is contented to let him or her to make an outward show of Religion, to go to the Church, to hear the Word, and to be able to talk thereof, as one that has written the Mystery of Witchcraft, * has by his experience observed.

---

* M. *Cooper*, his Mystery of Witchcraft.

For its very probable, that Satan deals not altogether with all his now, as he did once amongst the Heathen, and yet now doth amongst Pagans; nor as he did with the blind sots under Popery, or with some of the better learned in that kingdom of darkness; nor as he doth with some ignorant, silly, blockish people amongst us, incapable of the knowledge of the Truth and power of Religion: but that now, as he has taught his Grandsons, the Jesuits, to refine Popery somewhat, and to hide from their Proselytes in the entrance, the grossness of their Idolatry, to make them swallow down Popery at the first the more easily: so has Satan done in this Art of Witchery.

Or, it may be this, as Christ allowed some, which openly as yet did not follow him: to have power to cast out Devil's in his name, Mar. 9.38, 39, 40. who were not, as he said, against him, nor could lightly speak evil of him; so will Satan have some also, which shall not openly be his followers, but yet shall work by his power, and herein also imitate Christ.

If it be asked, 'Who these be, that thus are by a secret league workers by Satan?'

I answer in some sort, by way of similitude, from the direction of that place in Mat. 9.38 40. for Satan will be Gods Ape in all things whatsoever he can, and therefore will be also imitate, Christ herein.

1. They are such as invocate the Devil, by certain superstitious forms of words and prayers, believing that these means can affect what they have offered

them for, and do withal earnestly desire, to have them effectual. Now the Devil hereto consents, and affords his power, at the utterance of the words, to bring the thing to pass which is desired: Here therefore, is a covenant and mutual consent on both sides.

[*] For if a man or woman be content to use superstitious forms of invocation for help in time of need, and in using them, desires in heart to have the thing effected, if the Devil work the feat, there is a secret compact: for they have desired, and he has consented.

2. They are such as do know, that neither by Gods work in nature, nor by God's ordinances from his Word, the things they do, are warrantable, (but rather hear such things forbidden,) and that they also are absurd to common reason,[†] and yet will they do them, because they find an effect answerable to their expectation; As for example, to use Spells, and Charms, which are plainly forbidden by God, and against which many arguments are alleged by a learned man. Hereto add that which before I have mentioned: The healing of a wound by anointing the instrument which gave the wound, which Keckerman, both by reason and divinity proves to be Witchery, and shows that one Anselmus the Author thereof, was a very Witch.[‡] Many other Witchery tricks better

---

[*] Master *Perkens* his discourse of Witchcraft, chap. 2.

[†] Deut. 18. M. *Roberts* in his treatise of Witchcraft, p. 67. 72.

[‡] *Anselmus Parmensis. Deleio*, II. c. 4. p 24.30.

to be concealed, then named, many use, by which they suppose, to find help.

For if the remedy be not natural, then it is supernatural; if supernatural, then either from God, and so has warrant from his Word, and is ordinary, not miraculous; for that work of God has ceased long since; or else it is from the Devil, as the works wrought by Spells, [*] and Charms, superstitious prayers, and such like, forbidden by God, must needs be.

Therefore such do these things, are in a kind of league with the Devil, though ignorantly they think otherwise; because they are pleased to lay aside their reason, as men, to judge of a natural working, and their Religion as Christian men, in that they will do such things, which neither in themselves, nor by Gods ordinance, have any power to effect that which they go about to work by them; but only by the devil's power, who therefore is very well contented, to satisfy herein, their desire, and so is there between them a secret compact and league.

3. As those which in Christs name cast out Devils, though they openly followed not Christ, yet finding success in their attempts, were not against Christ, nor likely could speak ill of his power, by reason of their secret and implicit faith & Covenant with Christ: so these sorts of persons, finding their practices

---

[*] For vain & superstitious observations, see *Debio*, l. 3. p. 2. q 4. *Sect*. 2. pag. 446. 457.

successful, are not against Satan, nor can lightly speak ill of his working power, because of the secret and implicate league they have with him, and especially, because of the profit they find come to them thereby.

Quest. It may be here asked, why Satan will not urge these, to make a more open league?

*Answ.* It may be, besides the former reasons noted before, that he rests satisfied with this thought of them, that they are on his part, because they are not against him; as also he is content to let them please themselves with hope of Gods mercy, for that in thus doing, they suppose they sin not, nor are in danger of the Devil, nor under Gods wrath, as the other are, because they fall not so foully into the pit of destruction, by an express league, as the other sort do.

# CHAP. VIII.

*That there are such as be called good Witches,
and how they may be known.*

AS in Gods Church there be good and bad; So in this kingdom of Satan, there are good and bad Witches.

These good for white Witches are commonly called blessers, healers, cunning wise men; or women (for there are of both sexes) but of this kind, many men.

These have a spirit also, as one Joane Willimot acknowledged,* and are in league with the Devil, as well as the bad and black Witches be.

By their spirit they learn, who are bad Witches, and where they dwell, who are stricken, forespoken, and bewitched, and by them they learn how those do, whom they undertake to amend; for the spirit is sent unto their patients from them; all which the foresaid Jone Willimot acknowledged before Authority in her examination.

The profession of these Witches is, for the most part, to heal and cure such as be taken, blasted, stricken,

---

* In the Discourse of Witchcraft, against the E. of evil. children.

forespoken, as they use to speak, and bewitched: all which cures they do by their compact with the Devil.

But though these Witches be almost all healing Witches, and cannot do to man, or beast any hurt, except they procure some other to do it, yet we may find, that some of these sometimes have the double faculty, both to blesse, and to curse, to hurt, and to heal, as it is probable *Balaam* had, at the least in *Balak's* imagination, Numb. 22.6. For he ascribed to him the power of blessing & cursing, as had a famous Witch, one Hartley in Lancashire, and a woman Witch; of both which, Master Cooper in his Mystery of Witchcraft doth make mention. But, I say, for the most part, I find them curing Witches; some more obscure, and some more notable then others, as was the Sorcerer Simon Magus, who be witched the people so,[*] as they verily supposed that he did that he did, by the power of God. when the Text tells us, that it was by Sorcery, and so by the power of the Devil.

Their reward is for their curing, what people commonly will give them; some take more, some take but a little, often nothing, and some may not take anything at all, as some have professed, that if they should take anything they could do no good; of such an one Bodin makes mention, which went all in patched and ragged clothes. Here also the Devil will

---

[*] Acts. 8.

imitate Christ,[*] who said *Freely ye receive, freely give*.

The good Witches (untruly so called) may be sundry ways known.

I. From the quality of the party, one commonly very ignorant of religion,[†] an observe of times, of good & bad days, of good and bad luck, very superstitious in many things not enduring willingly such as fear God, and such as delight in his Word. They are also fantastically proud, as Simon Magus was, who boasted much of himself, as these do of their gift and power; as those in Spain, which call themselves *Salutadorres*.

II. By his or her unwillingness to confrere, either with godly and learned Divines, of their Faith & good prayers, by which they profess to do such cures, or with godly and learned Physicians, about such medicines as they prescribe to procure health: both which they avoid, lest their works of darkness should come to light, and they be discovered to be Witches.

III. By their private and secret whisperings, mumblings and mutterings with a low voice, as was the manner of Witches to do in old time, Isa. 8.19. & 29.4.

---

[*] In *Damono*. lib. 3. cap. 2.

[†] Deut. 18.

IV. By professing to be able to help such as be bewitched and forespoken: [*] for the supernatural work of the devil, as in case of bewitching, cannot be cured (as learned men affirm) by any natural means: this Witches have confessed also, and therefore must be by a league between the Devil and the Witch.

V. By the means which they do use to help such as come to them for help: as [†]By only touching the party: Bodinus gives instances, who thus cured the Ague & Toothache. 2. By saying certain prayers, as Anne Baker did,[‡] and Joane Willimot: which be Popish set prayers many of them; as so many Creeds,[§] Ave-Marys and Pater-nosters,[**] as a Witch confessed to me. 3. By Charms and Spells, absurd, barbarous and ridiculous forms of words, and such like means, which have no power from natural working, nor from the ordinance of God, and therefore must needs be from the Devil.

VI. By the remedies which these prescribe unto others to do, to have help, as[††] one or two medicines for all diseases, impossible in nature to be available in so great variety, and therefore do no good, and are prescribed only to cover their diabolical practice and

---

[*] Professions to help the bewitched. *Bodin.* in *Dem.* l. 3. c. 1. etc. 20. *Philo Iudeus.*

[†] See *Deleio*, Lab. 3. *cap.* I. etc.

[‡] Leicestershire Witches.

[§] Bodin, e 3.c..5

[**] The Lord's Prayer, especially in Latin, said multiple times.

[††] Our late revered Dioćelan B. L. kes, worthy of eternal memory said, this was a note of Witch if not a counterfeit.

Witchery. So to prescribe medicines made of such things, as are abhorring to nature, of which Bodin makes mention. [*] To prescribe Charms, popish prayers, popish superstitions, and very Witcheries themselves, as to hang Amulets about the neck, and certain pieces of holy Scripture, to go and scratch the suspected, to burn some of his or her hair, or some part of the beast bewitched, to prick a needle or bodkin under the stool where the Witch sits, to make a Witch-cake of Bakers meal, and the bewitched parties Vain: see for this and some others the like vanities, in Master Roberts practices, unbefitting reasonable men, and sober Christians.

VII. By their foreknowledge to tell who those be that come to them, why, and for whom they come. Thus could the Witch of Endor tell, that he that came disguised,[†] was Saul. Thus could he that made the Witchcake, tell the party which came to him to help his wife, of whom Master Roberts doth write. That such are Witches, Bodinus brings instances out of Flanders,[‡] Portugal, France. To tell also who are bewitched, and how, and who are Witches, and where their mark is; these be Witches: for all these things, they know by their spirit, as Joane Willimot the Leicestershire Witch did confess; part hereof in her first, & part in her second examination, before

---

[*] Bodin *Daemono.* lib 3. cap. 2. & 5. See Scot *of Witchcraft*, for Charms, Amulets, and other things, b. 12. c. 9.14 18. *Delrio* lib. I. c. 4.9.3, 4 His Treatise of Witcher. pa. 53.64.66 See Bodin. *Demo.* l.3. cap. 5. Foreknowledge.

[†] 2. Sam. 28.

[‡] Lib. 3. *Daemo.* cap. 5.

several Justices. For this foreknowledge, Physicians have not by their Art, neither have these ignorant persons this by divine inspiration, and therefore by compact with the Devil.

VIII. By showing the suspected in a Glass,* as he that made the Witch-cake did, before mentioned, who showed the Witch Mary Smith in a Glass. Fernelius speaks of such a Witch, whom he, as himself says, saw. This is an undoubted mark of a Witch, as one Master Edmunds of Cambridge told me, who was one that for a time professed to help men to goods or money stolen, who was once by the heads of the University questioned, as he confessed to me, when he had better learned Christ, and given over his practice that way. He told me two things (besides many others, in a whole afternoons discourse at Castle *hiningham* in Essex) never to be forgotten. 1. That by his Art he could find out him that stole from another, but not for himself. 2. That the ground of this Art was not so certain, but that he might mistake, and so peradventure accuse an honest man, instead of the offender, and therefore gave it over, albeit he said he might have made two hundred pound per annum of his skill.

IX. By pains and like torment coming upon this good Witch, which is upon the bewitched. Conference I had once with a suspected healing Witch, a man

---

* Showing one in a glass. Gifsard at his trial of Witchcraft, Fernel. l. 1 c. 11. Lode abdit. rerum causis. Read *Peter de Loier de spectris transt.* by Zach. Joannes, ca. 12. pa. 121.

miserable poor, and of a horrid countenance, of whom I asking how he knew a man or beast to be bewitched, he told me by two things. First, by his trouble in saying his prayers for the bewitched, which then he could hardly remember, and much ado he had to make an end of them; which prayers were so many Creeds, so many Ave-Marys, so many Pater nosters. Secondly, by the pain which would seize on himself as soon as he began his prayers, the very same which was upon the bewitched. This skill he learned of a woman, which taught him a secret, but what that ground of this Witchcraft was, that could I by no means procure him to reveal. Some know who are bewitched, as before I showed, by their spirit, & some by some Witchery means, of which Bodinus makes mention, and of many vain people yet put in practice,[*] when they suspect a party; for which they deserved to be punished, if they had their desert.

X. Lastly, by requiring Faith of such as come unto them: Physicians expect it not, neither dare any truly fearing God, rob thus God of his honor (who curses such as trust in man) and yet these Witches profess, that they cannot heal such as do not believe in them.[†] This Bodinus shows by examples three or four, whereof one Healer came to a Bishop, and willed him to trust in him to cure him, and this was in the hearing of Bodinus himself, there in the Chamber, and one

---

[*] Lib. 3. cap. 11.
[†] Lib. 3. c. 1. & 2.

Doctor Faber, a learned Physician. Thus may these, falsely so named good Witches, be discovered.

# CHAP. IX.

## *That none ought to go to these Wizards, Witches, blessers, healers, cunning men or women, for help.*

*That none ought to resort to these miscreants and cursed chastises, there be plenty of reasons.

1. The Charge and Commandment of God, forbidding the same expressly, Levit. 19. 31.

2. It is a spiritual defilement and Whoredom, for the Scripture faith, they go a whoring, Levit. 20.6. and are defiled by them, Levit. 19.31.

3. It is a dealing with the Devil, and seeking of help from him, as Ahaziah did:† for you have heard by the confession of a Witch, that such have a Familiar, and some have been known to invocate the Devil to cure another: And surely their mumbled, and senseless prayers, what are they, but watch words between the Devil and them? I knew one, that hearing a little boy greatly tormented in the next room where he was, went out into a back-side, and staying sometime there, returned in again, but yet in a great sweat, the boy that had cried a whole week, ceased presently

---

* *Delrio li*. 6. *Sect*. 1. q. 2. *pag*. 936.
† 2. Kin. 1.3. Bodin. lib. 1. cap. 6.

92

his crying: the Wizard prescribed (if the child felt pain again) a certain medicine of diverse herbs, which I had from the man himself: but over the head, and before he began to prescribe the medicine, these words must be written, as they were taken from his own mouth. *Onguint manera Iaiaanquintmanera*, very senseless; but in these words, were hidden the power of the medicine,* and were the watch-word between the Devil and him, to affect the work. Those therefore which go to these Wizards, seek help of the Devil.

4 It is a heathenish practice, to seek to such, Isa. 19. 3. & 65.4. 2. King. 17.17. Now we should not be like the abominable heathen,† in any evil, much less in these abominations.

5. They which seek unto them, are commonly wicked, and evil people, haunted themselves by an evil spirit, who suggests this course into them, as he did into Saul, 1. Sam. 28. yea, such as esteem of these, and think they work in God's name, and by his power, are bewitched in so thinking, Act 8.9, 11.

6. It is found true by daily experience, that those which most use them, most need them: for these Witches either breed, or nourish devilish and uncharitable conceits, in those that seek unto them:

---

* In many ancient books on medicine as well as a great many alchemical texts, the authors used obscure languages to conceal hidden meaning and secret messages within, meant only to be understood between others of the same craft.

† Je 10.2.

as that they dwell by ill neighbors; that when any ill happens unto them, to theirs, or to their Cattle, that they are blasted, taken with an ill planet, stricken, that some ill thing went over them, that they are over-looked, forespoken, and bewitched by someone or other, and therefore they must seek for help, and this must be of them, or of such as be like them, Wizards and Witches. By which speeches, and wicked counsel, they are continually kept on work in daily seeking to them, when any, the very least cross happens unto them, because they are ever imagining Witchcraft, and that the only remedy for help is, to seek unto these.

7. Learned men of all sorts generally condemn this running to these Wizards: Saint Augustine,* Saint Busili and Saint Chrysostom. Hippocrates a heathen, calls those Nebulones, which by Satanic means, profess to cure diseases, and says, (mark a Heathen's words) That God which purges the most desperate evils, is our deliverance. Some Schoolmen hold it to be an Apostasy, to seek and use help of Witches: *Aquinas*, *Bonanen*. *Albertus*, *Durand*,† cited by Bodin. *Master Roberts* cites the Lawes of Emperors, and the decrees against such. All the godly and learned Divines in our days do condemn the same,

---

* Lib. 10. de civit. Dei. In pg. 45. In hom. 7. ad Colossenses. King James in *Daemon*. l. 3. c. 5. In his treatise of witchcraft. p. 61. 62. See all that have written on the Com. Exod. Levit. Deut.
† *Scot*. b. 12. c. 18. & b. 16. c. 3. *Bodin*. l. 3. c. 2. & 5.

the dead by writing, the living *vina voce** in their Sermons.

8. They often lose their labor, for sometimes the healer is but a *Counterfeit Witch*, (worthy severe punishment for deluding people:) And though a Witch, yet can he, or she do nothing, but by the Devil's help, and he himself has confessed to the Witch, that he cannot cure that sometimes, which at the bad Witches instigation he has inflicted. Again, Satan, though he has his healers, yet must they live one by another: therefore he heals for one Witch, one or two diseases, for another more, not for one all, and this, as it happens by their conditions, in the bargain-making with the Devil, when they enter into league with the Devil. Sometime this white Witch cannot cure the bewitched, without the consent of the bad Witch, which caused it, or (which is fearful to think upon,) till the same disease be put upon some other, or that the Witch be bewitched to death, which has inflicted the torment upon the diseased party. All these *Bodinus* noted, with examples cut of *Sprangerus* an Inquisitor that examined, [†] had the confessions, and put to death great numbers of Witches.

These Witches, to keep their credit, often deliver their medicines with an If: *If it does no good, come again*. When they return and find that the Devil has

---

[*] Voice blame

[†] See in Scot, book 12 chap. 7. a notable cozening trick of such a Witch, to make her speech true in accusing an honest woman, for a Witch.

not removed the disease, or that God being displeased, will not let them; then the Wizard's blame them, that they came not in time, or they applied not the means aright, or that they wanted faith to believe, or at least they acknowledged their power not great enough, and therefore they advise them to go to a more cunning man or woman, and so direct them unto another Witch, or Devil, for help, worse than themselves.

9. And lastly, * the Lord threatens to set his face against that soul, and to cut him off from amongst his people, that seeks unto them.

Let these reasons dissuade us therefore, from helping ourselves by such detestable means so abhorred and hated of God.

---

* Levit. 20.6.

# CHAP. X.

### *That many yet run unto these Witches, and their reasons which they allege, answered.*

There is no action so bad, but if men either get, or save thereby, there will be both the practice, and the approbation thereof, ever by some: so are men captivated to the care of a bodily safety, and preservation of an outward estate in this life. So it happened in this case, of going unto, and seeking help of Witches, who use such reasons as these, to countenance their going to them.

I. *Such surely work by God, because they use good prayers, and good words, and often name God.*

But to answer this, let them remember that the Devil himself can use good words, Mar. 1.24. and 5.7. Act. 17. that he can counterfeit the habit and words of a holy man Samuel, 1. Sam. 28. 13, 15, 17. that he can turn himself into an Angell of light, 2. Cor. 11. Therefore, he can teach his servants to feign holiness. As for their prayers, they are foolish, popish, superstitious, if not all, most of them, and some of them learned of the Devil himself,[*] as some have confessed.

II. *That they use ointments, herbs and medicines to cure the diseased.*

I answer, 'These are but colorings to cover their Witchery.'

1. Because they use but one medicine, and the same commonly to cure many diseases.

2. Because they cannot cure any disease, but that which is by cherie, and therefore they say, that such persons, or that thing is bewitched, for which the comers to them seek remedy, showing hereby what diseases they can cure. Therefore, natural medicines to cure supernatural diseases, are used only to hide their Witchcraft, and sorceries.

III. *That it may be, as some think, that they have a gift from God, this way to do good.*

*Answ.* There is no reasonable probability for this, for then God would not condemn them, nor such as seek to them: neither would he suffer his servants to be so afflicted, (as you have heard) in using his gifts; he would not so ill reward his servants: and this conceit of being the power of God, was in the bewitched Samaritans, who thought so over-well of Simon

---

[*] *Bodin*. l. 3. c. 5.

Magus, as these Samarian-like bewitched people do of these silly Ma-gooses.

IV. *That they have endured great torment, and great losses of cattle, and could not otherwise find help.*

*Job* was in another manner tormented, and received far greater losses, yet he depended upon God, patiently waited his leisure, resolved to trust in God, though he should have died, and therefore was at length delivered. A woman which had a disease *twelve years*, & had spent all she had, under the hands of Physicians to be cured, but could not, but rather grew worse, yet she resorted not to diabolical means (that we read of) though ordinary means failed her, but waited God's good time, and was miraculously delivered, Mar. 5.25. 29. So another woman had a spirit of infirmity, and was bound by Satan *eighteen years*; yet she would not (for anything we know) use any ill means for her help: for the Text says; *She was a daughter of Abraham*, Luk. 13. 15, 16. and therefore was at the length also cured.

V. *That many have gone to such, and found present remedy.*

1. As some have found remedy, so other some have not, even by your own testimony; so set one against the other. 2. The lawfulness of an action is not to be judged by the success. Wicked men in ill ways prosper sometimes, to the hardening of their heart in evil, and so is there a spiritual plague upon them for their wickedness, which they do not consider of. 3.

We have the Apostle's lesson.[*] *We may not do evil, that good may come thereof*: the going to them God forbids, and therefore evil: and bodily ease will not excuse the sin before God.

4. Let such consider what before is delivered, touching such as be hoped, whether they continue well, or whether a worse evil has not after befallen them, or whether the like has not happened to some of theirs, or to some of their cattle, or to some of their friends, as stories show, that so it has happened, and so it may still fall out.

VI. *That they have help from these at a little or no cost at all, whereas Physick is very chargeable.*

But let such consider, that physical means is of God, in the use whereof we may pray for a blessing; whereas this is of the Devil, and the remedy with a curse. We cannot, we may not pray to God to find remedy in seeking to the Devil. It's also a miserable sparing, to spare the purse, and to damn the soul.

VII. *That these speak against bad Witches, and often discover them, and therefore cannot they themselves be bad.*

This is no good argument; for he may be bad enough himself, that sneaks against another, in something worse than himself. As for the discovery of a bad Witch, you have heard by the testimony and

---

[*] Romans. 3.8.

confession of a Witch, that this they do by the Devil's telling: Therefore being in league with the Devil, they are for all these pretexts to be detested, and their villainies before God to be abhorred.

# CHAP. XI.

*That there are bad Witches; and here of their profession, and practice, and how many things must concur in bewitching anything.*

All Witches, in truth, are bad Witches, and none good; but thus we distinguish them, after the vulgar speech: It is needless to make particular proof of this sort: History, experience, and confession of such Witches are evidence enough.

Of this sort are men, but very many women, younger, and older, but almost all very miserably poor, the basest sort of people, both in birth and breeding, most incapable of instruction, and cursedly negligent, and profanely condemners of the saving knowledge generally, people they are of ill natures, of a wicked disposition, and spitefully malicious against any with whom they are displeased, eagerly pursuing to be revenged.

The profession of these is, by the Devil's instigation, only to do hurt. To do mischief is their common practice: yet some of them also (as with the white Witch) the Devil dispenses with,* to help, as well as

---

* The trial of Lancashire Witches.

to hurt, as the Lancashire Witch *Chattox* could by he own confession: and that old Mother Witch *Dembdike*, as other Witches at the Barre confessed of her.* So could *John Samuel* the Witch of *Warboys* bewitch and unbewitch, as his wife confessed: and examples of these *Bodinus* gives.

All these Witches have Devils and familiar spirits, as is evident by the confession of a multitude of Witches; those in Lancashire, Leicestershire, Bedfordshire, Northampton shire; by others in France, Germany and other places; so as this is a truth not to be doubted of.

These spirits appear in sundry shapes, yea the same spirit to the same party in diverse forms, as *Chattox* Devil called *Fansie*, would be sometimes to her, like a brown Dog, sometimes like a Man, and sometimes like a Bear, as she confessed.

These spirits are received of one from another Witch,† as *Joane Willimot* had a spirit by *William Berry* her Master, who received it by his blowing into her mouth. This *Joane* afterward helped *Ellen Greene* to two spirits. Many such instances may be brought.

But the Devil uncalled comes and offers himself to most, as he did to *Dembdik*, to *James Deuice*, to *Lewis Gaufredy*, and infinite others. Some call for

---

* In the arraignment of the Witches of Warboys In *Daemono*. I. 3. c. 5.

† Discovery of Leicester Witches.

one by name, through the persuasion of another, as once a boy at Bradley calling Bun.[*] Bun, looking up to the thatch of the house, there leapt a Toad to him, which went up to his crown, and sucked. Some Witch calls spirits to give them to others, when before they have drawn them to consent to have them, as the forenamed *Willimot* did, called *Pusse* and *Hiffe*, and gave them to *Ellen Greene*. Some Witch teaches another to use some ceremony to have a spirit, as to go to the Sacrament, and bring away the bread, and to give it to the next thing which they should meet, as old *Dembdike* advised *James Deuice* to do:[†] or to go about the Churchyard, and to kiss whatsoever they meet. By these, and many other such like ways these common Witches come by their spirits: for of other Magicians I speak not here.

By these damned spirits do these cursed caitiffs[‡] work all their malice and mischief. For these they call, when they would do harm, as far as these spirits have power to do hurt, and then bid them do this or that for them. Thus, *James Deuice* willed *Dandy,* his spirit, to go and kill *Mistress Townley*. *Elizabeth Deuice* the Mother, called *Ball*, her brown dog, to kill *John Robinson*. *Chattox* called for *Fansy,* her dog, to go and bite one *Moore's* Cow to kill the same.

For these spirits can do great mischief,[§] if God permit, many ways. They can work upon the mind of men

---

[*] In Wiltshire

[†] Lancaster Witch.

[‡] Cowardly person

[§] *Delrio*, l. 2. q. 9, 10, 11, 12, 13, 14. In his life and death.

and women to stir up lusts and ill passions. *Gaufredy* had a spirit to stir up lust in any he breathed upon.[*] *Philip Flower* had a spirit,[†] to make one *Thomas Simson* to love her: other instances *Master Roberts* does give.[‡] They can make men and women mad and frantic, as *Mary Smithe's* spirit did *Edmund Newton*. They can annoy the body many ways; the relations of the trial and arraignment of Witches, are full of variety herein. They can kill both man and beast,[§] and blast corn, and do many other evils and harms: needless it is to take up time with instancing particulars: they can bespot linen clothes with pictures of Toads, Snakes, and other vermin; as the spirit of one *Hellen Jenkenson* did a Buck of clothes of *Mistress Moulshow*,[**] because she had the day before helped to search the Witch, and found the mark upon her. Thus they work by their spirits, and else by themselves can effectuate nothing: neither can the spirits do anything without God's permission.

For this we must know,[††] that three things must concur in the bewitching of one man, or any other thing whatsoever.

1. Before any of God's creatures can be annoyed, he must give way and permit the same: this all will grant,

---

[*] In his life and death.

[†] Leicester Witch.

[‡] In his *Treatise of Witchcraft*. Roberts pag. 57, 58.

[§] *Delrio*, *lib*. 4. part 1. q. 3. *sect*. 2.3, 5.

[**] Northampton shire Witch.

[††] *Delrio*, *lib*. 3. p. 1. q. 1. pag. 354.

who acknowledge a divine power and providence of God ruling and disposing of all things.

II. Then the operation of the Devil, according to the power of God permitting, which he knows either before, as is clear in the story of *Job*, Chap. 1. and 2. also by the relation touching the Witches, which bewitched the E. of *Rutland's* children; where we may read, how *Joane Flower*, called for, and willed *Rutterkinne* her Cat, to go and mischief the *Lady Katherine*, and the Cat cried Mew, and thereby showed the Witch, that she could not do her any hurt. Or the spirit knows not before, but when he has gone and made trial, and then finds his power limited, as we may read in the relation of the Warboys Witches: how *Mother Samuel* sent two of her spirits against *Master Throgmorton* and his wife, who making trial what they could do, returned, and told her, *That God would not suffer them to prevail.*

III. Before the spirit work for any Witch (though he will go for himself, and of himself, where he has no league with the Witch) yet to do for her or him, he will not, without their consent and will, to make them guilty with him. The Witch therefore must do something to set him on, as to call him, to bid him go, to give him something before he go, as an old Witch gave him a Cock: of which we may read in Master *Gifford's* Dialogue of Witches. So they send, but the Devil doth the harm, and not they.

Nevertheless, they are made guilty of these mischiefs. 1. Because they call them and bid these spirits do such evils. 2. Because they speak, and do such things as please the Devils, and which they desire and counsel to have done, while they themselves go about and do the mischief, (which though the Devils can do) yet will they not do it for them, without these watchwords, and signs. 3. That they think verily, that they have given them power to do the mischiefs, laid to their charge, and thereupon they confess, they hurt such and such persons, or killed this or that man or beast. 4. Because they assume to themselves, a kind of glory within themselves, when the people fear them, and they have a joy in their hearts, that they can awe others so by such thoughts of them. 5. And lastly, by the Covenant made with the Devil, they think, that what he doth, is done by their commanding power over them, and that they must so do, because they will have them to do so.

For these reasons may the Devil's deeds be imputed to them: and they may be said to do, what the spirits do, though their own words and deeds have no force in them of themselves, to effect their wills; albeit Satan makes them believe otherwise: but herein are they notably deceived, as also when they think themselves to have him at command to do their pleasures: for,

1. The spirit will do more sometimes, then the Witch would have him. For *Agnes Samuel* a Witch of *Warboys*, entreated the spirit Blue that Mistress *Joane Throgmorton* might not have any such extreme fits: but she could not prevail with him.

107

2. He will not undo that sometimes which the Witch wishes to be undone again, * as the Witches of *Warboys*, all three, endeavored to unwitch the Lady *Cromwell*, but could not.

3. He will threaten the Witch, and offer some violence unto her, if she will not do what he would have her, as the spirit did old *Dembdike*, † who showed and pushed her into a ditch, because she would not go and help *Chattox* the Witch (whom *Dembdike* could not abide) to make pictures. So *Chattox* spirit threw her down, because when he appeared, she would not speak unto him. Yea, ‡ *Bodinus* tells us, that when one called his spirit, and then did not set him on work, he presently killed him.

4. He will annoy them, as he did Mother *Samuel*, tormenting her in her body grievously:§ & as he did *Chattox*, taking her eye-sight from her, yea, and would sometimes come gaping upon her in the form of a Bear, with open mouth, as if he would have worried her, as she confessed.

5. He will discover the Witches practices, and will endeavor to bring them to their confusion and end: as the spirit told Master *Throgmorton's* children in their fits.

---

* Dod in l. 3. c. 2. p. 247.

† Lanc. Witches.

‡ In his book *de Daemono*.

§ Torment them; Warboys Witches.

*6. And lastly, he will fail them, and break promise with them, in their greatest need; as he did a famous Witch in *Hungary*, after she was in prison, where wanting food, did then eat her own flesh and perished.

Thus we may see, how little command they have over spirits, but as the spirits lift, for their own advantage.

---

* Roberts in his Treat. of Witchcraft, p. 79.

# CHAP. XII.

## To know whether one be bewitched, and the signs thereof.

God permitting, and the Devil working at the Witches command,[*] man or woman, beasts or other creatures may be bewitched.

Now, to know who are bewitched, what course better can be taken, then to gather the signs from such as certainly have been known to have been bewitched, and that by the confession of Witches arraigned and condemned for the same: as,

When learned and skillful Physicians can find no distemper in the body, or any probable reason of any natural cause of such grief, pangs, and violent vexations, as the patient in the judgment of all the beholders doth endure: as Master *Throgmorton's* child did, when neither Doctor *Barrow*, nor Master *Butler*, learned Physicians, could yield any sound reason of; as to sneeze loud and thick, almost half an hour together, till blood come out of the nose and mouth: to have a great swelling, and heaving in the belly, then a passing to the throat ready to stop her breath, to make one speechless, and set the teeth

---

[*] *Delrio.* l. 6. c. 2. *Sect.* 2. q. 3. p. 969.

together, to shake sometimes the leg, sometimes the arm, sometimes the head, as it were a fever or some running palsy,* to thrust out ones arm so stiff and straight, as not possible to bow it, and such like motions as befell those children.

When some parts of a man, now fingers, now toes do rot, and no rules of Art, or experience can do any good, but rather the worse, by the best means; or if seeming in the Evening to be healing, † in the morning to be found to have gone backward, as it did with one *John Orkton*, bewitched by one *Mary Smith of Linne*.

When a very healthy body on a sudden shall feel violent torture, pinching at the heart, bereaving him of sense, and so distract the patient, as he or she is ready to tear the hair of their head, as it befell one *Elizabeth Hancock*, bewitched by the forenamed *Mary Smith*,‡ or being in health, strong and travelling by the way, to be suddenly taken, and to fall down lame, become speechless, lose the use of one side save the eye, to have the head drawn awry, the face and countenance deformed, hams lame and turned out of course, feeling within prickings, as with Elsons and Sickles, as did one Abraham Law, bewitched by one *Alizon Deuice*, meeting him by the way.

---

* paralysis

† Roberts his Treatise.

‡ Relation of Lancashire Witches.

When two or more in the same family, or dwelling asunder, one or more in one town, and othersome in another, are taken in the like strange fits in most things, as were Master *Throgmortons* children, the Lady *Cromwell*, who had visited those children and burnt some hair of the suspected Witch: So was Master *Avery*,* and his sister one Mistress *Belcher*, dwelling in several places: for such violent strange fits cannot come upon natural causes, so suddenly alike to diverse persons, in so several places, except some infectious disease should happen among them, to take it one of another.

When the afflicted party, or parties in their fits, do tell truly many things: some things past, as the elder daughter of Master *Throgmorton* did, who told what the Witch had been doing. Some things *in doing*: as she told where her uncle and others were in the Towne: where the Witch was, and whither going, what they said and did when they met her. These sisters could tell in their fits, in what case and state one and another were, at the same instant, being 8.10. or 12 miles asunder, and also when the Witch fed her spirits, and what she said unto them, as Mistress *Joane* could tell some things to come, as in her first fit, how many in that house should be bewitched, and named the number and persons: Also the other (as well as this sister,) told what the Witch Agnes Samuel would do, if *M. Throg*. would go and speak with her; they foretold their fits in their fits, how many afterwards, and how long they should hold

---

* In Northampton shire.

them: that Mother *Samuel* should willingly confess her fault, and the time wheñ. All these proved very true: yet these things are no effects of natural diseases.

When one shall do many things, sneeze, scratch, groan pitifully, start fearfully, heave up the belly, bounce up with the body strangely, become senseless, not hearing, seeing, or feeling: to speak also many things to purpose, and yet out of the fit to know not anything hereof: as it happened with these children.

When there is strength supernatural, as that a very strong man shall not be able to keep down a child of nine years old upon a bed. So it was with one of Master Throgmorton's.

When the diseased do vomit up crooked Pins, Iron,* Coals, Brimstone, Nails, Needles, Lead, Wax, Hair, Straw, or some such like things; such have been seen to have been vomited up: as Doctor *Cotta* witnesses and produces the witnesses for the same,† and those learned men.

When (with other things concurring, else this is no sure sign) any do see, not in a fancy or dream, but visibly some apparition, and thereupon some mischief to befall them: as it did to one Master Young of London, the appearance of a Waterdog to

---

* pag l. 2. c. 8 221.
† In his trial of Witches. *Delrio, lib.* 3. *par.* 1. q. 4. *sec.* 6. pa. 410.

run over his bed;[*] and at another time one clothed in russet, with a bushy beard, speaking to him. So also Toads and Crabs, crawling about his house, after which he was tormented.[†] So Master *Averie*, whom before I have mentioned, saw as he rode in his Coach homeward a vision, and forthwith his Coach-horses fell down dead. One Master *Engersmen* in Bedfordshire, driving a Cart of corn to Bedford, saw a great black Sow grazing, which went along with them: at length the horses brake their carriage, and ran away to Bedford: so at the returning back they saw the same Sow, and had the like violent course of horses: the chief man, afterwards, by a stroke of a Beetle upon his breast, fell into a trance suddenly, and was in his senses distracted, and continued for a long time in ecstasies and grievous perplexity.

To these may be added what formerly is written of the signs of such as the Devil torments; for what he can do without the association of a Witch, that can he do when he is willed by the Witch to do his work. And thus, much briefly for these signs of persons bewitched.

---

[*] M. Roberts Treatise, pag. 57.59.

[†] In the discourse of Witches executed at Northampton.

# CHAP. XIII.

*What those things be which Witches do,*
*by which they do set their spirits on work*
*to do mischief, and by which they are*
*said to bewitch.*

Though as you have heard,[*] Witches do not the harm themselves, yet do they that which the spirit will have them to do, before he will work the mischief.[†] He sets them on, puts into their hearts evil thoughts: he inflames them with rancor, yea and appears visibly speaking to them, counselling and urging them to do this and that; before he doth the hurt, they agree; and so the Witch sends him, who is ready enough to go of himself, but he will not, in cases of Witchcraft.

That which the Witches do, are as *Watch-words* and *Signs*, that the Devil may know, as it were, when, where, and upon whom to do mischief. The means which they use, are diverse, and many, by which (as we commonly speak) they bewitch man, or beast.

---

[*] See *Cotta*, p. 89 90, 91. *Delrio, lib*. 3. *par*. 1. q. 1. pa. 354▪ q. 2. q. 3.

[†] The truth of these things appears in relations of Witches' confessions.

*By *cursing and banning*, and bitter imprecations: this is very usual with such: and the Devil encourages them thereto, as he did one *Mary Smith* of *Linne*, the effect whereof fell on *John Orkton*, whose fingers she wished might rot off, when he was strong and well, and so they did, and his toes too afterward.

By threatening with curses: as *Chattox* the Lancashire Witch did one *Hugh Moore, Anne Nutter* and others, who died thereupon.

By *Charms & Spells*, [†] the words whereof being repeated, the Devil will do hurt. *Bodin* mentions how a maid could get no butter, when a boy repeated a verse, till he was made to pronounce it backward again. By a Charm did *Gaufredy* bewitch one *Louise Chapeau*, into whom the Devil entered.

By *certain forms of words like prayers*, using the name of God and the Lord Jesus, or the Virgin *Mary*, whom they call our Lady; seeming hereby to call upon them for a blessing, they use these as a *Watchword* for their spirits, as when they say, *Here is a good horse*, *God save him*, etc.

By praising and by words of commendations:[‡] this *Bodinus* confirms by many testimonies: and *P. de Loyer de spectris*,[§] who cites *Au. Gellius* his *Noctes*

[*] M. *Roberts, pag.* 46.
[†] *Lib*. 2. *cap*. 1. Scot, b. 12. ch. 16 & 17. In the summary before the admirable History of the Magician.
[‡] *Lib*. 2. *cap*. 4. *Lib*. 9. *cap*. 4.
[§] The specters of Loyer

*Atticae* for the same: whereupon the Italians hearing any to praise others very much, say, *Di gratia no gli diate mal d'ochio.*[*]

[†]By their looks, if with an intent to hurt: thus could one *Gamaliel* Greet do, into whom while he was swearing, a spirit like a white Mouse entered, as *Joane Willimot*, the Leicestershire Witch confessed before authority.[‡] *Bodinus* also mentions this kind of hurting, and *Virgil*, in this verse, *Nescio quis oculis, teneros mihi fascinat Agnos.*[§]

[**]By their breath, as a Witch in the Diocese of *Constance*, who blowing, infected the whole body of a man with Leprosy: so did *Gaufredy* bewitch with his breath.

By touching with the hand or finger, as *Ellen Greene*, one of the Leicestershire Witches, touched one *John Patchett's* wife and her child in the Midwives' arms, and then sent her spirits to witch them to death.[††] For the spirit *Dandy* said to the Lancashire Witch *James Deuice,* wheñ he went to one Duckworth's house, Thou hast touched him, and therefore have I power over him. A Witch touched but the breasts of a

---

[*] Do not pray to give an earache

[†] *Delrio*, l. 3. *par*. 1. q. 4. *sect*. 1. In the story of the Earle of Rutland's children.

[‡] *Lib*. 2. *cap*. 4.

[§] I do not know who to the eyes, the soft and cast on my tender lambs.

[**] *Bodin*. l. 2. c. 8. In the book of his life and death.

[††] Confessed in his examination.

woman that gave suck, and dried up her milk: this *Danaeus* witnesses, [*] *Mary Sutton*, a Bedfordshire Witch, did but touch the neck of one *Mr Enger's* servants only with her finger, and he was presently after her departure miserably vexed.

By *making pictures* of Wax and Clay of those which they would bewitch, [†] and either roast them, or bury them, that as they consume, so will the parties; a notable story hereof is in *Boëtius* of one King *Duff*, [‡] a Scottish King, which is recorded fully in the Chron. of Scotland, The Lancashire Witch *Chattox*, and some others were much exercised in this Devilish practice, as their confessions in their examinations do witness. *Joane Flower*, which bewitched the Earle of *Rutland's* children, would curse the Lo: *Rose*, and take feathers and blood & boil them together, using many Devilish speeches and gestures, as her daughter *Philip* confessed.

By tying of certain knots, as Saint *Jerome* testifies in *vita Hilarionis*.

By *sacrifices*, as *Balaam* attempted: and as a woman before-named did offer a Cock, and another a Beetle (as *Serres* in the French Chronicle witnesses in Henry the 4. days) or some the very paring of nails, or but a piece of a girdle, as a spirit asked of the forenamed *Joane Flower*.

---

[*] *In Dial. de Soruarijs.*

[†] *Delrio*, l. 4. *par*. 1. q 4. *Sect*. 4. *lib*. 2.

[‡] See *Scot*. b. 12. *cha*. 16.

By *getting something* of those whom they mean to bewitch: So the Witch Flower got the right hand glove of the Lord *Rosses*, which she first rubbed on the back of her spirit *Rutterkin*, then put it into hot boiling water, after taking it out, pricking it often, and wished that the Lord Rosse might never thrive. There was a Boy at Bradley, which a spirit in form of a *Toad* called *Bun*; which spirit as he confessed, told him, that to kill a man's horse, which he rode to the water, he must get the Owner to give him something, as Bread & Cheese,[*] or what else, before he could kill him.

By the Witches *giving something*, as enchanted powder, ointment, herbs, yea, or apples, or strawberries, bread, cheese, drink: this has been found true many times.

By these (and no doubt many other ways) they work to affect their wills, and do bewitch others.

---

[*] Aust. in Ciuit. Dei. l. 18.

# CHAP. XIV.

## *Who they be that are most subject to be hurt by these bad Witches: and of the remedies against Witchcraft.*

[*]Though God may try his dearest children this way, yet it is very seldom, and upon their goods rather than upon their bodies: yet sometimes it has been found, that they have prevailed to the taking away of the life of some, who have been reputed religious.

Such as usually & most commonly are plagued by them, are,

1. *Carnall Gospellers*, such as profess religions, without the power of religion, *Newtrals, Time-servers*, very *worldlings, Libertines, Profane, Only Outsides, Lukewarm Laodiceans*,[†] and such like.

II. *Grossly superstitious*,[‡] *heathenish observers of times*, of good or bad luck, or unlucky days, being dismayed at signs, as at the power of Planets: so

---

[*] See Master *Cooper* his Treatise of Witches. Lib. 2. *cap*. 1. *sect*. 4.

[†] In reference to the Loadicean Church

[‡] Jer. 10.2. For superstitious observations. See *Delrio*, l. 3. *par* 2. q. 4. s. 3, 4. p. 447, 459.

when they stumble at first going out at the doors, when they meet with a splay-footed woman, or a Hare crossing them, when they put on 1. hose or shoo before another, as the left before the right, their bleeding suddenly at the nose, their burning of their ear or cheek, right or left, the falling of salt, the croaking of Ravens, the chattering of Magpies, with a thousand of other heathenish observations.

III. Such as upon any manner of cross are easily led away to think themselves bewitched: for wee commonly find where people least suspect such, there is the most freedom from such.

IV. Those that most fear them, whom they do suspect to be Witches, and for fear does give something unto them. For such are often paid home for this their fear of man, when (it may be) in their course of life, they fear neither God nor Devil, but live very licentiously.*

The verity of these things will appear, by observing commonly such as be bewitched and by considering what manner of persons they be for the most part.

Therefore, to prevent the power of Devils, & whatsoever Witches can do, let us labor,

1. To entertain and uphold the preaching of the Gospel. For where it comes, down goes the power of Witchery, Act. 8. & 13. Histories tell us, where the

---

* Extravagantly

Gospel came amongst the Heathen, there this hellish power of Devils and spirits, greatly diminished:[*] as in Norway, and those other Northern coasts. And do we not see, that where the Word is faithfully preached, and people obedient thereto, how these places are, either not at all, or very rarely troubled with Witches? Where Popery and profaneness is, with contempt of preaching, or vile neglect thereof, there such miscreants are rife.[†] *For surely there is no Enchantment in Jacob, nor any Divination in Israel.*

II. With outward means labor to bring forth fruits worthy the Gospel, and amendment of life: for God hedges the virtuous man about, Job 1. so as Satan cannot come at him, without very special license from God, and that only for a trial: The Angels of God do also pitch their Tents about such, Psal. 34. yea, and have charge over them to keep them in their ways, Psal. 91.11, 12.

III. To have holy and Religious duties in our families, to pray with them rising up, and lying down, and to lift up our hearts in holy and heavenly ejaculations in our going out, and in performing the duties of our particular callings: For, *Pray continually*, says the Apostle, 1. Thes. 5. And Saint *James* tells us, that the prayer of a righteous man avails much,[‡] if it be fervent. *David* did not only serve God openly in the Tabernacle, but returned home, to blesse his house,

---

[*] Bodin. l. 3. c. 1. p. 230.

[†] Num. 23.23. In or against either reading.

[‡] James. 5.16.

2. Sam. 6.20. And *Job* every day sacrificed to God, and sanctified his children and family, Chap. 1.5. And God gave to Israel a Law to sanctify their houses.

IV. To go ever well-armed against these rulers of darkness, Devils and evil spirits, furnished with the heavenly furniture and spiritual weapons, of which the Apostle speaks, Ephe. 6.14, 18.

V. Being thus qualified, and thus armed, to trust in God only, who will keep you under the shadow of his wings, Psal. 91. and fear no Witches, nor Devils; knowing ever this, that they cannot do the very least harm to any of the least creatures of God, without leave from him: no, not to enter into the Swine of the very *Gadarens*. Therefore rest on him, and when any cross happened, say with a holy subjection *to his will, It is the Lord, let him do what seems him good*, 2. Sam. 15.26. *It is the Lord that gives, it is the Lord that taketh away, blessed be the name of the Lord*, Job 1.21.

# CHAP. XV.

*Of the means which have been used by diverse to help themselves, when they think they, or anything they have is bewitched.*

\*IT is a miserable thing to see the vanity of people in so clear light of God's Gospel, how they run yet, either to unlawful, or to weak and very uncertain means, to relieve themselves in cases of suspected Witchcraft, as these and such like; for I will recite only the most usual.

I. To run to a White Witch, and to seek help so from the Devil, and to put in practice his or her tricks of witchery (of which before) to drive away a Devil, and to help the bewitched: an ungodly course as before is proved, and accursed before God.

II. To beat the suspected, as Master *Enger* did *Mary Sutton* the Bedfordshire witch, upon which, his servants were well; so one *William Fairborn* did bear *Anne Baker*, the Leicestershire Witch, whereupon his

---

\* Of Charms and other detestable remedies used by vain people, see *Scot.* b. 12. *chap.* 21.

son *Thomas* recovered and amended. Sometimes such effects follow after, but we must remember,

1. That this is not ever so, as fell out with one *Henry Mills,* who had ill nights after.

2. Except it be by the appointment of the Magistrate, it is against the Law of man, and being a private revenge, is against the Law of God.

3. This then being evil, we may not do it,* that good may come thereof, it's no means of God's appointment.

4. The torment upon the party is by the Devil, which sometimes the Witch cannot remove, if she would: the three Witches of *Warboys,* would have unwitched the Lady *Cromwell*, but could not: if she does, it is by making a prayer to him; of which *Bodin* gives a fearful example of a Witch,† praying to the Devil, to cure one whom she had bewitched: And if the Devil does cease to torment, it is because he would nourish this revenging practice against both God's Law, and against the Law of the land; we may not violently inure others, because they have hurt us.

III. To burn something of the Witches', which, what effect it may have to heal the bewitched, I know not, nor upon what ground, either in natural reason or in religion: but this I am sure of, that when the Lady

---

* Romans. 3.8.

† Li. 3. c. 5.

Cromwell, made some hair of Mother Samuels to be cut off, and her hair lace with it to be burnt, the children of Master *Throgmorton* were not the better, and the Lady was bewitched soon after, so as when Mother *Samuel* had tried her husband, and after, her daughter to unwitch her, they could not. For they may send their spirits to do mischief, but it appears by this, that the Devil, except he lists, is not at their command to help and heal the party.

IV. To fetch the suspected,* and to *scratch* him or her to get blood, as one Master *Avery* and his sister did scratch two Witches, and drew blood of them at Northampton, & presently found ease: but this must we know,

1. That albeit they had a little ease, while the Witches were with them, yet they were no sooner out of sight, but he and she were in their old fits, and more vehemently tormented then before. This is then no certain remedy.

2. It is no lawful remedy, no more than beating the suspected. Violence upon private motion, is a revenge, and we may not offer it to another, to ease ourselves.

3. This is a remedy which the Devils themselves have confessed to practice, † & which the Devil has strengthened some to be able to do: as you may read

---

* In the trial of the Witches at Northampton.
† The Warboys Witches.

in the Relation of Master Throgmorton's children in four several places, especially of one Mary, a little child, kneeling on her knees, [*] who scratched the young Witch a big maid, whilst the child was in her fit, and said that the spirit bade her do it; that the spirit willed her not to pity the Witches crying, that the spirit held down the Witch to her, that it forced her to scratch, stretching forth her arms, and straining her fingers, whether she would or no, to do it. Is this a good and Christian remedy, wherewith the Devil is so well pleased? Neither for all the scratching did the children amend, but were again in their fits, and that often afterwards. Yea I have read, [†] that a woman Witch willed voluntarily one to scratch her to help him.

V. Some in the fits bring in the suspected, and make the same to *Touch* the *afflicted* party.

This may be used, but yet no resting thereupon: for,

1. I have showed, that by touching they bewitch people: the sign is therefore uncertain.

2. By the suspected's presence, though sometime the afflicted has had ease, as was proved in Master *Throgmorton's* children often; yet in that relation we find two things: First, that at Mother *Samuels* presence, when Mistress *Jane Throgmorton* began her fits, she grew worse, and the rest fell into their

---

[*] The child was but 9. years old.
[†] See Gifford's discourse of Witches.

fits at another time, as soon as they saw her. Secondly, that the said Mother *Samuel*, when she perceived afterwards, that the children were the better for her being with them, made a new composition with the Devil, that they should be ill when she was with them, and this the children in their fits revealed openly. So that the Witches presence or absence is but a very uncertain means, seeing that is of no force either way, but as they make their league with the Devil: for there is no natural reason for it, nor divine ordinance.

There was another trial used very often by *M. Trogmorton*, to bring his children out of their fits, which was this: to make the Witch to say, *I charge thee, thou devil, as I love thee, & have authority over thee, and am a Witch, & guilty of this matter, that thou suffer this child to be well at this present*: and by and by the child should be well.

But here note, that the Story tells us, that one of the spirits was the author and counsellor to this, and told one of the children in her fit, that if *Agnes Samuel* were made to speak these words, the child should for the present be well. What warrant they had to take the Devils instruction, and to make her use these words, so cursed & fearful, I leave to the judgment of the wise and religious.

VI. Some go to them, and threaten the suspected, to carry them before authority, to prosecute law against them, and to hang them; & thereupon some have been well.* *Bodinus* gives diverse instances hereof.

†This may be used: they may be threatened with the course of justice, to make them fear.

But this is no certain remedy: for some Witches are so far from being hereby moved to cease their Witcheries, as on the contrary they are the more provoked to evil, as was *Mary Smith* of Linne, who being threatened by James Scot, that he would hang her, if his wife had any such fits, as aforetime she had, did soon after bewitch her again, & she was tormented as formerly she had been.

This and such other like means people do use for ease & help, but they are either uncertain or unlawful. The best is *Fasting and Prayer*,‡ to remove a devil, as before has been delivered: for God only can free us from Devils and Witches, and his means appointed must we only use, and therein expect from him a blessing.

---

* L. 2. c. 1 & l. 2. c. 5.
† Roniglus in *Daemonolatria*, l. 3. c. 3.
‡

# CHAP. XVI.

*That Witches may be discovered, though there be many difficulties therein, and the causes thereof.*

IT is not to be doubted, but that Witches may be detected; this is certain.

1. From God, in the giving of his Law against Witches, Exo. 22.18. *Thou shalt not suffer a Witch to live*. Which implies a discovery of them, or else it could never be put in execution, and so should be a law to no purpose.

2. From History: First divine: for *Saul* found our Witches, and executed the Law upon them, 1. Sam. 28. And so did good *Josias*, 2. Kin. 23.24. Secondly, we have Chronicles and many relations made of the evident discourse of Witches.

3. How trials in our own country at many Assizes.

So as it is clear that Witches may be discovered, though it cannot be denied, but that there are some difficulties therein, and that for these reasons:

I. Because of the secrecy of the grounds of Witchcraft so close and hidden, as being one of the greatest works of darkness committed this day under the Sun.

II. For that from natural causes may arise very strange tortures, pangs and torments, as if the afflicted were bewitched in the judgment of most ordinary apprehensions.

III. Because of cunning counterfeits, who can so lively express the outward & visible appearances of such as are bewitched, as if they were indeed really possessed & bewitched.

IV. For that witnesses may feign their accusations, yea and confirm them by oath to be true: of which we have a notable example of one Grace, or rather graceless, *Sowerbutts*, enticed by a Priest or Jesuit called *Tomson, alias Southworth,*[*] to accuse her own Grandmother, her Aunt, and another woman, all three Protestants, of Witchery, and that she had by them been afflicted, and seen them in their practices of Witchery, in the night, sometimes in one place, & sometimes in another, naming when, where and how, and the ground of all this was, because they would not become, forsooth, Roman Catholics: a bloody practice, fit for a Romanist, and very unnatural.

V. Because of the strong imagination of such as suspect themselves to be bewitched, which will make them think verily that they see strange apparitions; and for fear will dream of the suspected, and so may

---

[*] In the trial of the Witches of Lancaster.

cry out and talk of him or her in their fearful dreams, the fantasy being oppressed. And if the disease called the *Mare*, happen to such a one, then their sweating, their moving, and struggling, with an imagination of one creeping upon them, from the feet to their breast, (they awaking in fear and trembling) will make them say and swear too, that they are bewitched.

VI. For that vain persons many times are the pursuers of the suspected, who are so transported with rage and uncharitable desire of revenge, (they still fearing some harm by them, except they can rid them out of the way) that they will over-diligently gather matter to strengthen their suspicions: some out from mere imagination; some from words & deeds taken in the worst sense; some from the sight of some creature on a sudden, as a Cat, Weasel, Polecat, or such like, late in the evening, where they saw not any before; some from idle relations of superstitious neighbors; some from accidents happening upon others, upon a suspected person, and (their falling out; & if the pursuers be of some ability, to these shall be added the too confident avouching of some flatterers, that such an one is a Witch, and all tending to further the rage of the pursuer, to bring the suspected to his or her end.

VII. Because there may concur many seeming probabilities, which commonly mislead many for want of judgment, and for want of thoroughly weighing the weight of them in such a case, taking such presumptions for sufficient proof, when they are nothing so.

VIII. And lastly, for want of deep search into the subtlety of Satan, who (as is proved) often works without any association, or league with the Witch: yea (as is also before declared,) the diseases or death of men or beasts may be merely natural, and no work of Satan therein at all, and yet even in these things he has his mischievous devices, to make them to be cast upon some man or woman, altogether innocent of the same and thus he doth it.

He knows when his power is granted him of God to do hurt to man or beast, also he knows the growing of a natural disease in man or beast: he knows the ripening thereof, & at what time it will break out. Now mark, before his own act, or that in nature break out, he stirs up some occasion to make the party, man or woman, to be afflicted in their persons, or cattle, to fall out with some angry neighbor, man or woman, either immediately, or some small time before; that so this act of his own, or of nature may be imputed unto that angry waspish-natured & shrewd-tongued neighbors, so come to be reputed a Witch: which he having gained by two or three such pestilent practices, he sets wicked people on to follow such an one to death, that innocent blood may be shed, & many become guilty thereof, which he thirsts after. A mischievous subtlety of all the wise-hearted *Grand-Jury* Gentlemen seriously to be considered of. And this should make angry malicious natures, such as be given to cursing, railing and bitter speeches, to be reformed, even in this respect, lest God punish them, by giving them over unto this bloody practice of Satan, to their shame and destruction.

For these reasons it happens, that it is a hard thing to discover the practices of Witchcraft, without more diligent search, then is commonly used to detect Witches.

# CHAP. XVII.

*That there are some great presumptions of a Witch, for which he or she may be brought before authority to be examined.*

*I Will not here trouble myself to set down the many surmises of people that such & such are Witches, because they be the vain conceits of the addleheaded, of silly fools, or of rattling gossip, or of superstitiously fearful, or of fanciful Melancholiacs, or of discomposed and crazed wits, as a Divine speaks. But here I will set down such probabilities, as may justly cause the suspected to be questioned, as these:

I. To be much given to *cursing* and imprecations, upon light occasion, and withal to use *threatening* to be revenged. And presently thereupon evil to happen, and this not once, or twice, to one or two, but often, and to diverse persons.

This is a great presumption (all these circumstances withal considered) because Satan offers himself (as before is showed) unto such, and such means, we find that Witches use to bewitch men and beasts; yet

---

* Of weak conjectures. *Delio*, I. 5. *sect.* 4

is this but a presumption, for that many are so bitter spirited, that they will curse & ban, & threaten revenge, and yet be no Witches. Also Satan is subtle, as is noted in the former Chapter, to make use of God's leave given to himself, and of the working of natural diseases, which upon cursings break out, as is caused thereby.

II. An implicit confession, when any come & accuse them, for vexing them, hurting them, or their cattle; they shall hereupon say, *You should have let me alone then*: as *Anne Baker* a Witch, said unto one *Miles*: or, *I have not hurt you yet*, as Mother *Samuel* said to the Lady *Cromwell*, when she caused her hair to be burnt: or to say to one, *I will promise you that I will do you no hurt*, upon this or that condition, as others have said. These kinds of speeches are in manner of confession of their power of hurting, and yet but a presumption; because such speeches have been, and are used upon diverse occasions, by others which are no Witches.

III. The suspected's diligent inquiry after the sick party, and an over-inquisitiveness to know how such an one doth, falling sick presently upon his or her cursing and threatening, with the suspected's coming to visit him or her unsent for, especially after they be forbidden the house. Thus have those done which have been found condemned for Witches: yet but a presumption, because man's heart being revengeful, and having cursed and threatened, and hearing of some sudden mischance, is so taken up with a cursed joy, as makes him or her thus to do, and yet by no league with the Devil. For *Solomon's* words may not only be applied to Witches, but even to all others, as an inbred evil in man's heart, *Rejoice not at the fall of thine enemy*. And fore coming being forbidden, it is the impudence of some of the poorer sort, rude and ill-mannered to do so, and to bring some small thing to curry favor again.

IV. The naming of the suspected in their fits, and also where they have been, & what they have done here or there, as Master *Throgmorton's* children could do,[*] and that often, and ever found true. This is a great presumption; yet is this but a presumption; because this is only the devil's testimony, who can lie, and that more often than speak truth.[†] Christ would not allow his witness of him in a point most true: nor Saint *Paul* in the due praises of him and *Sylas*.[‡] His witness then may not be received, as sufficient in case of one's life. He may accuse an innocent, as I showed before out of M. *Edmunds* giving over his practice to find stolen goods. And Satan, we read,[§] would accuse *Job* to God himself to be a hypocrite, and to be ready to be a blasphemer. And he is called the *Accuser of the Brethren*.[**] Albeit I cannot deny, but this has very often proved true: yet seeing the Devil is such an one, as you heard, Christian men should not take his witness, to give in a verdict upon oath, and so swear that the Devil has

---

[*] Relation of Warboys Witches.

[†] Mark. 1.25.

[‡] Acts. 16.

[§] Job 1.

[**] Revel. 12.

therein spoken the truth. Be it far from good men to confirm any word of the devil by oath, if it be not an evident truth, without the Devil's testimony, who in speaking the truth, has a lying intent, & speaks some truths of things done, which may be found to be so, that he may wrap with them some pernicious lye, which cannot be tried to be true, but must rest upon his own testimony to ensnare the blood of the innocent.

V. An apparition of the party suspected, whom the afflicted in their fits seem to see. This is a great suspicion: for some bewitched have cried out, seeing those who were suspected to be Witches, and called upon them by name, as *Mistress Belcher* in Northampton shire, of *Joane Vaughan*, *M. Engersman*, or *Mary Sutton* of Bedfordshire. So did *M. Throgm*. children upon *Mother Samuel*:[*] yet this is but a presumption, though a strong one: because these apparitions are wrought by the Devil, who can represent unto the fantasy such as the parties use to fear, in which his representation, he may as well lye, as in his other witness. For if the devil can represent the Witch a seeming Samuel,[†] saying, *I see God's ascending out of the earth*, to beguile *Saul*; may we not think he can represent a common ordinary person, man or woman unregenerate (though no Witch) to the fantasy of vain persons, to deceive them and others, that will give credit to the Devil?

---

[*] *P. de Loyer de spectris.*
[†] 1. Sam. 28.

VI. The common report of neighbors of all sorts, if withal the suspected be of kin to a convicted Witch, as son, daughter, brother, sister, niece, or nephew, or Grandchild, or a servant man or maid, or of familiar acquaintance with such an one. This is a cause of suspicion: For common reports of near neighbors of all sorts do arise out of some shows, and Witches are known to endeavor to make others Witches, such as they daily converse with, as Mother *Samuel* of *Warboys* did her daughter: old *Dembdike* the Lancashire Witch did her grand-daughter, & grandson, her daughter and a neighbor of hers; yet all this is but a presumption; because a common report may arise, though not upon no grounds, yet upon very weak grounds, being duly examined: and though witches do labor to make others like themselves; yet we find, when Mothers have been executed for witchery, some of their children have not only been no Witchery miscreants, but by God's mercy, have become religious and zealous Christians, of which I could give some instances.

VII. The testimony of a Wizard, the cunning man or woman; this may be a great presumption: for who can better discover a Witch, then a witch? and many have been found such, whom the Wizard has accused to be Witches. But yet, this is but a presumption; because, if he be not a counterfeit (taking upon him to know more then he doth) but indeed a very Witch; yet is his testimony sometime the testimony only of the devil, by whom he comes to know another to be a Witch, and not upon his own knowledge; and though in this case he be found to speak true sometimes, yet may he lye also, being instructed by the father of lies.

But as concerning this Witness, if a Wizard happen to cast out of himself an accusation against another without asking, it may be used for a presumption: but none may go to such an one to ask his testimony, nor use his skill to discover a Witch, no more than for this end, to go to the devil himself.

To use a sieve and a pair of sheers, with certain words: To put something under the threshold, where the suspected goes in, or under the stool where he or she sits, and many such witchery tricks and illusions of Satan to be detested.

To burn some clothes in which the sick party lies, for to torment the Witch; to burn part of the creature in pain; to burn alive one, to save the rest; & to make the Witch to come thither: These are execrable sacrifices made to the devil, to be abhorred of all true Christians.[*] The Romans in old time put to death such as by Magick would discover thieves, to come by their goods stolen. Christians then should abhor these abominations. Some think it lawful to try one suspected, by casting him or her into the water, and bind their arms across: and if they sink not, but do swim, then to be judged Witches, as M. *Enger* tried upon *Mary Sutton*,[†] the first time bound as before, and then she swam like a plank: then was she

---

[*] Bodinus in *Daemo*. l. 3. c. 5.

[†] In Bedfordshire.

searched, and the mark found; and by counsel given him, she was the second time cast into a Mill-damn very deep, thus bound; her right thumb to her left toe, and her left thumb to her right toe, who sate upon the water, and turned round like a wheel, as in a whirlpool, yet they had her tied in a rope, lest she should have sunk.

But Doctor *Cotta* doth by many reasons,[*] dissuade from this trial, as not natural, nor according to reason in nature, and therefore must come from some other power, but not of God: for that were a miracle, which we are not now to expect from God, and therefore this strange work is from the Devil. The objections made he answered fully. There needs no miraculous means more to detect Witches, then other secret practices, and it is an adulterous, and unbelieving generation to look for a sign: and what is this but a presumptuous expectation of an extraordinary revelation from God without warrant? Of other unlawful trials, see *Delrio, lib.* 4. *c.* 4. *sect.* 6.

---

[*] See also against this, *Delrio*, l. 4. c. 4. q. 5. Sec. 3. pag. 655. In his tryall of Witches. cap.14. See M. Perkins against this in his discourse of Witchcraft, cap. 7. Sect. 2.

# CHAP. XVIII.

*Of the main point to convict one of witchcraft,
and the proofs thereof.*

TO convict any one of witchcraft, is to prove *a league made with the Devil*. In this only act stands the very reality of a Witch; without which neither she nor he (howsoever suspected, and great shows of probability concurring) are not to be condemned for witches. Without this league, they be free, though the Devil hurt men's bodies, kill their cattle, and that ill haps fall out, upon his or her cursing.

This is the principal point to be enquired after in all enquiries; this must be only aimed at; all presumptions must tend to prove this, and to discover this league; without which, no word, no touching, no breathing, no giving nor receiving, are of force to bewitch any.

If this be not proved, all the strange fits, apparitions, naming of the suspected in trances, sudden falling down at the sight of the suspected, the ease which some receive when the suspected are executed, be no good grounds for to find them guilty of witchcraft, and to hang them.

This league therefore, though never so secretly made, is to be discovered; seeing it is that only which makes a Witch, & by which all is done, which justly can be laid to her or his charge.

Now, they that make this league, have a Familiar spirit. For this is true, as soon as the league is made, the spirit, one or more, is familiar with them, as before is proved. This was proof sufficient of a Witch in Saul's, and Josias' time.[*] Then Witches were known to have familiar spirits: and such have they now, by which, after the league made, they work all their mischiefs.

Now the Witch thus in league and familiarity with the Devil, is convicted by these Evidences:

[†]1. By a *Witches mark*, which is upon these baser sort of witches, and this by sucking, or otherwise by the Devils touching, experience proves the truth of this, and innumerable instances are brought for examples. *Tertullian* found this true, & says, *It is the Devils custom to mark his*: *God has his mark for his*, Ezek. 9. Reu. 7. & 14. *The Beast will have his mark*, Re. 13. (who is the Devil's Lieutenant) so the Devil himself will have his mark: see the relations of Witches, & the witness of many learned men, writing of Witches

---

[*] 1. Sam. 28. 2. Kings. 23.24.

[†] Lib. de Coro. milit. & Bapt. See Bodin. De Michaelis his desc. of Spirits. Annot. Perkins and others. Delrio, lib. 1. p. 130. l. 2. p. 198.

and witchcraft. Therefore, where this mark is, there is a league and a familiar spirit.

Search diligently therefore for it in every place, and lest one be deceived by a natural mark, note this, from that. This is *insensible*, and being pricked will *not bleed*. When the mark therefore is found, try it, but so as the Witch perceive it not, seeming as not to have found it, and then let one prick in some other places, & another in the mean space there: its sometimes like a little *teat*, sometimes but a *blueish spot*, sometimes *red spots* like a flea biting, *
sometimes the *flesh is sunk* in and hollow, as a famous witch confessed, who also said, that Witches cover them, and some have confessed, that they have been taken away; but, says that Witch, they grow again, and come to their old form. And therefore, though this mark be not found at first, yet it may at length: once searching therefore must not serve: for some out of fear, some other for favor, make a negligent search. It is fit therefore searchers should be sworn to search, and search very diligently, in such a case of life and death, and for the detection of so great a height of impiety.

II. By *Witches words*: as when she or he has bene heard to call upon their spirits, or to speak to them, or to talk of them to any, enticing them to receive such Familiars, offering one, and counselling to do something to get one. Also, when they have been heard telling of the killing of some man or beast, or

---

* See the *life and death of Lewis Gaufridus*.

of the hurting of them, or when they have not only threatened revenge upon any, or their cattle, but have foretold particularly what shall happen to such a one, and the same sound true, and their boasting afterwards thereof. Furthermore, if they have been heard to speak of their *transportation* from home to certain places of their meetings with others there,[*] of which transportation stories make mention: and also the relations of the Lancashire Witches meeting at Malkin Tower, some 20. together, and were carried by spirits in likeness of Foals, as those Witches confessed.

These speeches are to be inquired after, & who can witness them: for they prove the league and familiarity with the devil.

III. By the Witches deeds, as when any have seen them with their spirits, or seen to feed some creatures secretly, or where the Witch has put such, with the smell of the place, which (as very learned men do avouch, & is found true by experience) will stink detestably. Also, when it can be found, that they have made Pictures (as the Lancashire Witches did) hellish compositions,[†] or any such Witchery Arts, as is before mentioned, cha. 13. Moreover when they give anything to any man, or other creature, which immediately causes either pains, or death.

---

[*] Bodin. his *Daemono. Detrio*, lib. 2. q. 16. de disq. magicae.

[†] *Delrio*, in *disq. mag.* li. 2. par. I. q. 4. s. 4.

IV. By the *Witches ecstasies*, which some of them have been found in, of which *Peter de Loyer*,[*] in his book *de spectris*. gives lively instances, with which the delight hereof Witches are so taken, as they will hardly conceal the same, but will tell it to one or other; and if they do not, it cannot be, but at one time or other they will be found therein.

V. By someone or more *fellow Witches*, confessing their own witchcraft, & bearing witness against others, so as they can make good the truth of their witness, and give sufficient proof thereof: as that they have seen them with their spirits, or that they have received spirits from them; that they can tell, when they used Witchery tricks to do harm; or that they told to do harm; or that they had done; or that they can show the mark upon them; or that they have been together in their meetings, and such like, as the Lancashire Witches gave testimony one against another of these things.

VI. By some *witness of God* himself, happening upon the execrable curses of Witches upon themselves, praying God to show some token, if they be guilty, as fell upon Mother *Samuel* the *Warboys* Witch, who by bitter curses upon herself, seeking to clear her self, wishing some sign to be showed, if she were guilty, presently her chin did bleed, the very place where her spirits did suck, as afterwards she confessed. So one *Iennet Presto*, a Yorkshire witch, was brought to the dead body of one M. *Lister*, bewitched by her to

---

[*] Cap. 12.

death, which she no sooner did touch, but the corps bled fresh blood. Such an evidence sometimes, though not always, is given from God, when he is so pleased to detect such malefactors guilty of blood.

VII. By the *Witches own confession* of giving their souls to the devil, and of the spirits which they have, and how they came by them.

If any think that it is almost impossible to make Witches confess this much, they are deceived; for I find by Histories exceeding many to have confessed, and in our own Relations of arraigned and condemned Witches, wherein I find how a Witch has confessed the fact, to the afflicted, being brought unto him, and charged with bewitching him: as *Alizon Deuice* did to *John Law*. So *to the afflicted friends*, as did Mother *Samuel* to M. *Throgmorton*. Some to Justices, when they were examined, as did the Lancashire and Rutland Witches. Some to the Judges so freely, as made the Judges and the Justices to admire thereat, as they did at Lancaster. Some in terror of conscience, truly apprehending the fearfulness of their league made, as did one *Magdalen* a French Gentlewoman, seduced by *Lewis Gaufredy*, who also himself at length made a large confession before his death.

We see therefore, that Witches may be brought to confess their Witchcraft. And thus much for the sound evidences, more than presumptions, upon which they may be found guilty, and justly be condemned, and put to death.

147

# CHAP. XIX.

## *Of the manner of examining Witches.*

There is required great diligence, wisdom and circumspection in the examination of a Witch. It was fit and necessary for such as be in authority, and have Witches brought before them, that they should be men, in some sort, well seen in treatises of witchcraft, to know how to proceed understandingly in detecting them, & to be able to judge wheñ the witnesses speak to the point.

That which the witnesses speak in this case, may be reduced to three heads.

1. To *weak conjectures*, which are commonly alleged by the weaker sort, arising out of their own imaginations, or idle speeches of some others. All of this kind the wise examiner may draw together, to make so of all, perhaps, a presumption; and in hearing the suspected parties answer to these, may collect matter of more weight.

2. To *strong presumptions*, such as are before set down, cha. 17. which are much to be insisted upon

3. To sufficient proofs, of which in the former Chap. last before.

The proof of the first, if no further presumptions can be made, may cause a watchful eye over the suspected, & do deserve a sharp admonition from authority, that the party take heed for increase justly of any such, though light suspicions, for the time to come, and so to send her or him home again, if the Law will permit.

The second sort, which are great presumptions, being justified by some witnesses, are just cause of the suspected's imprisonment, and are worthy, after trial at the barre (though not of death) yet of very severe punishment for the same, such as the wisdom of the Judge, and the laws will allow of.

But good evidence for the third, makes the party or parties justly guilty of death, and they ought to dye for the same.

Now, concerning the parties to be examined, they are many and in this order to be brought in, and that apart, & not in the hearing one of another.

1. Is the *afflicted party*, if he or she can come to give testimony. This party is to be questioned in these things:

1. How, when and where, and upon what occasion the pain happened to him or her? 2. How they be in their fits? what understanding or memory they retain, and with what apparitions their minds be troubled? 3. How the fit ends, and how they be after the same? By these may be gathered the natural or supernatural

quality of the disease. 4. Whether they have had the judgment of some learned and judicious Physician, touching the nature of the disease? 5. Why they should think the disease to come by Witchcraft, and not rather, either to be a natural disease, or Satan's work, through God's permission, without any league with a Witch? 6. and lastly, who it is they do suspect, and upon what good grounds?

II. Are the friends, father, mother, brethren, sisters and such as are near, and daily attend the afflicted in their fits?

1. The same questions may be demanded of these also.

2. They are to be questioned in the presumptions very thoroughly, as they be, in chap. 17. Lastly, whether any search has been made, to find the mark? If they have searched and found any, then how they know it from a natural mark? If search have not been made, then to command some fittest for the purpose, to make diligent search.

3. Are *indifferent neighbors*. But some are fearful, superstitious, or children, or old silly persons, whose testimonies are to be heard, but not easily credited, as being persons in such a case as this is, very much subject to mistaking.* Other neighbors, such as be of

---

* See *P. de Loyer in lib. de spectris*, his many reasons hereof.

understanding, well advised and conscionable, are to be questioned, and their testimonies regarded.

In questioning of these, it is to be demanded, 1. Whether they have seen the party or parties in their fits, and how often? 2. What the life and course of such has been? 3. What they think of the disease, whether natural, or by the devil, or whether the party doth not counterfeit, and their reasons every way? 4. What they think of the suspected party, his or her life and conversation? 5. If they suspect any, then upon what grounds? And here inquire of them the presumptuous, and the more evident proofs.

4. Are *suspected adversaries*, either to the afflicted, or to the suspected Witch. Though ill will, we say, never speaks well, as being willing willfully to mistake: yet is ill will desirous to find matter, and will pry very narrowly into everything, to discover what they desire to find. Therefore, though it be wisdom to suspect ill will, yet may some things be found out by them, which otherwise may be mistaken, or lye hid.

Inquiry may be made of these: 1. Touching the afflicted person, what his conversation is; and whether there be any probability of counterfeiting? Then concerning the suspected, what he or she is, and why thought to be Witches?

5. The *Physician*, if use have been made of him. It is very necessary to have his judgment in this case, to know whether the disease be natural, as he upon

mature deliberation, and diligent search has found it? or whether there be any counterfeiting herein? or if the disease be not natural, yet whether Satan may not mix with it his supernatural power, beyond the force of the disease? These are for Physicians to judge: And therefore it is very requisite to have the advice of some judicious Physician herein.

6. The report of a *White or good Witch*, as the people call him or her. This Witch must be brought before Authority, and it must be demanded of him or her, 1. What they have reported of the suspected party? 2. Upon what grounds they have thus accused the said party? for such an one may know the other to be a witch, one of these two ways: 1. Either upon some inward acquaintance; and so either by sight has observed, or by conference has learned so much from the suspected, or 2 By his own familiar spirits, as before I have showed by example in chap. 8. in one *Joane Willimot.*

Now, if such a one be a Witch indeed; he or she can discover the other, and can tell where their mark is, what be their practices of Witchcraft, & so is able to convince the other of the crime. Therefore such a witness in these things must be diligently examined. And if he or she cannot bring sufficient proof to make the accusation good, such a one deserves severe punishing, for their speeches against the suspected.

VII. Are the *suspected Witches whole family* able and fit to answer, and to give evidence, also such as be known to have had inward familiarity with the suspected? These upon the parties present apprehension, are to be brought before Authority also, and forthwith, upon their attaching, to be kept asunder from the suspected, and one from conferring with another, except it be openly heard what they say: for these of all other are most likely to be able to detect the suspected, in his or her secret sayings, or doings. At their apprehension, then also to search the house diligently, for pictures, or powders, bones, knots, pots, or places where their spirits may be kept, ointments, and for haircut, books of Witchcraft, or charms, and such like.

These are to be examined, 1. of the suspected's cursing and threatening. 2. Of his or her much inquiry after the afflicted party, how he doth; and when he or she began to be so inquisitive; as whether, upon some present falling out, and after his or her cursing and threats? 3. In hearing the party to be ill, whether he or she boast anything, or rejoiced thereupon, with the reasons thereof? After the examination of these presumptions, then to inquire further:

1. Whether they have seen him or her call upon any spirit, or to speak of it to them, or to have seen them feeding them, or found any secret place to be suspected, and giving forth a noisome and stinking smell?

2. Whether they have heard the suspected to foretell of mishaps to befall any, or heard them speak of their power to hurt this or that, or of their transportation,

to this or that place, or of their meetings in the night there? or known them to have used charms or spells?

3. Whether they have seen them with any other suspected of Witchcraft, and to have secretly received anything from them, and what it was? To have made any pictures? or to have used any other tricks of Witchcrafts? See *Delrio, l.* 5. *s.* 3. *p.* 711.

4. Whether they have desired to have something belonging to the afflicted, before the same party were afflicted? or whether the suspected he or she did get anything, to send or to carry to the foresaid afflicted, and what fell out thereupon? and what the suspected did at his or her return;

5. Whether they ever found the suspected in any ecstasy or trance, when & where? & what he or she has told them thereupon afterwards?

6. What he or she has been heard to say or do upon the afflicted? his or her crying out of the said suspected in the fits or trances; & of his after accusing the suspected out of the fits? whether before hearing they should be apprehended, fear of death surprised him or her, and being apprehended, if he or she sought to get out of the way?

Now, while these sorts are in examining, it was very good, in the mean space, to have a godly and learned Divine, and somewhat well read in the discourses of Witchcraft and impieties thereof, to be instructing the suspected, of the points of salvation, of the damnable cursedness of Witchcraft, and his or her fearful state of death eternal, if guilty and not repentant. That thus by God's blessing, in the Ministers instruction, and his earnest praying for a blessing before he begin, the suspected may be happily prepared to confession before Authority, when he or she is examined.

VIII. After all the rest, is the *suspected* to be examined, but alone also at the first, from the hearing of all the other witnesses, or examinants.

The examination of this must be according to the answers of the others, and their proofs & reasons, & that in the order as they were examined, & to make this suspected to answer distinctly to every of their testimonies against him or her.

In thus orderly examining him or her suspected to mark his or her down-cast looks, [*] fear, doubtful answers, varying speeches, contradictions, cunning evasions, their lying, or defending of this or that speech and deed, or excusing the same. Also to observe, if any words fall from him or her, tending to some confession, as to say, If you will be good unto me, I will tell you, &c.

And whether he or she can be brought to shed tears, [†] or no: for it is avouched by learned men, upon experience in many trials of Witches, that a Witch indeed, will hardly or never shed a tear, except God

---

[*] *Delrio*, l. 5. *Sect*. 4.723.
[†] *Delrio, lib*. 5. *Sect*. 4.726, num. 25.

work the grace of true repentance, which will appear by a free confession.

If after this examination alone, he or she will not confess, then to bring the witnesses, one by one, to his or her face, to just fie their former testimonies; and to hear his or her answers again, and to mark how they either agree or disagree from the former.

If none of these will work to bring them to confess, then such as have authority to examine, should begin to use sharp speeches, and to threaten with imprisonment and death. And if the presumptions be strong,[*] then if the Law will permit (as it does in other countries in this case) to use torture, or to make a show thereof at least, to make them confess, as many have done hereupon in other Countries.

But this extremity shall not need, if thus an examination be made, as it ought to be, and withal, that prayer be made to God for a blessing in proceeding thereto; as once in France, upon the examination of that grand Witch *Lewis Gaufredy*,[†] before noble Commissioners? One of these being (as the story says) zealously affected, when he perceived how cunningly the Witch by his answers sought to blind the eye of Justice, and that they could not catch him; he entreated the rest to pray with him; which having been done with one accord, the wretch in his answers was so confounded, as he was taken in his

[*] *Delrio*, l. 5. *Sect*. 7. p. 735.
[†] See his life and death.

own words, and so by God's hand, being thereto enforced, he fell to a full confession of his fearful Apostasy from God; and so was condemned and burnt alive, as Witches be there.

# CHAP. XX.

## *The holy Scriptures do condemn all sorts of Witches.*

The distinctions of Witches into good and bad, is only according to the use of speech amongst the people: for Witches are all bad, and condemned by God, not only for that they do hurt, but because they are Witches.

Yea such Witches God doth condemn, as abomination to him & to be rooted out, as men of all sorts both heretofore, and yet now too many, are over favorable unto: this is clear and manifest many ways: as

1. By the words of the Law, where it is said, *Thou shalt not suffer a Witch to live:* as if it had been said, *If thou shalt find one that is a Witch*: though such an one as thou could be contented to wink at, and to pass by (as people now do such as be called with us, good Witches) yet shalt thou not suffer him or her to live; no more than a bad Witch: If a Witch, then ought he or she to die for the same.

II. By the examples of all recorded in the Scriptures, whom we find to be such kind of Witches, as got credit and estimation, love and liking (as good Witches do, and not as the bad, hatred & ill will) with

Potentates and great persons in the world, as did the Magicians & Sorcerers with *Pharaoh*, [*] with *Nebuchadnezzar* & *Balthazzar*. As did also Simon Magus with the Samaritans, who was held to be the great power of God, Act. 8. likewise *Elymas* was with *Sergius Paulus*, and the *Pythoness* with her masters,[†] Act. 16.

Such they were, as by great persons were sent for, as those in Egypt and Caldea. Such as they would make use of, as *Balak* did of *Balaam*,[‡] as *Manasseh* did of Wizards, and as *Saul* did of the Witch of Endor. Such they were, as many of the people (as ours do too, to good witches) sought unto, inquired after, Jer. 27.9. resorted unto, yea and counselled one another to seek unto, whom they heard and believed, as they did their false prophets. To these they had regard, and after these, as the Scripture speaks, they went a *whoring* Such they were as were openly known among the heathen, as among the Egyptians, Exo. 7. Canaanites, Deut. 18.12. Philistines. Isa. 2 6 & Chaldeans, Dan. 2 & 5 & also amongst the Israelites, as appeared by their resorting to them, and yet these God utterly condemned, howsoever men esteemed of them.

III. By all the means given unto them, by which these sorts are set forth, & rather such as be now held good

---

[*] Exo 7. & 8. Isa. 47 12. Ezek 22.21. Dan 3.7.

[†] Act. 13.

[‡] Num 22. 2 King. 21.6. 1. Sam 28. Isa. 8.19. Jer. 27.9. Levit. 19.31. & 20.6. Isa. 19.3.

Witches, then such as be held cursing and bad Witches.

1. Is *Chosem*, Deut. 18.10. 2. King. 17 17. which comes of *Chasam*, *Futura praedixit.* * a Diviner foreshowing things to come. Such, people delighted in, and consulted with, Jer. 27. 9 Ezek. 21.26. Such a one was *Balaam*, Ios. 13.22.

2. Is *Megnonen* or *Gnonen*, Deu. 18.10. *Gnanan, Nubem abduxit*, this is called a Soothsayer *excontemplatione coeli, aut nubium, eorum{que} colore & motu aliquid praedicere: obseruator nubium*: A gazer on the heavens, and from the Clouds to foretell something. To these did the people give ear, Jer. 27.9. and such an one was *Manasseh*.[†]

3. Is *Menachesh*. Deu. 18.10. Of *Nachash*, *explorauit*,[‡] *Scrutator*,[§] a searcher out, *qui dies vel hor as explorat*,[**] & so conjectures and foretells. An Observer of times, to know when it is best to begin a business, as *Haman's* Witches did,[††] by casting lots before him.[‡‡] Of this *Manasseh* also was guilty.

---

* Predicted future
[†] 1. Chron. 33.6.
[‡] Discoverer
[§] Examiner
[**] Latin: That day or hour as he explores
[††] Hest. 3.7. & 9.24.
[‡‡] 2. Chr. 33.6.

4. Is Mechashshepth, Deut. 18.10. Isa. 47.12. of Chaphash, *Magiam exercuit*,* a Magician, one that can deceive the eyesight, by making something appear to the sight, otherwise then it is: Such Pharaoh called to him to oppose Moses, those two, *Iannes* and *Iambres*, of whom St. *Paul* speaks: and hereof also was *Manasseh* guilty, 2. Chron. 33.6.

5. Is *Choreb*, Deut. 18.11. of Chabar, *consociatus est*: an Enchanter, or Conjurer: one joined in league with another, as the Witch is with the Devil: Such an one used charms to tame Serpents, Psal. 58.6. Many such were in Babylon, Isa. 47.9. This is the same that Lachash is, Eccl. 10.11. *Incantation. Gils Ob*, Deut. 18.11. Levit. 20.27. one which has a spirit, in Hebrew is called *Ob*, which in him or her does give answer to such as come to inquire of them: such a one was the Witch of Endor, 1. Sam. 28, *Quaeritè mihi mulierem; babentem Ob, or Pythonem*:† Such a one was the *Pythoness*, which brought her Masters much gain, Act. 16. Such as have this spirit within them, make answer out of their belly, of things past, present and to come, to such as come to enquire of them; their bodies being swollen like a bottle: or speaking low, as out of the ground, a whisperer, Isa. 29.4. and hereupon he or she is called *Ventriloquus*.‡ To such the people had regard, Lev. 19.31. and encouraged one another thereto, Isa. 8.19.

---

* Practitioner of magic
† Find me a woman nearby Ob or Python >>?
‡ Greek Omitted.

7. Is *Iidgnoni.* Deut. 18.11. of *Iadang, nouit*, a Wizard, 1. Sa. 28.9. one also that can foretell things, and so called for his or her knowledge, as now we term a Wiseman, such a one a wise man, or a wise woman. After this sort the people also sought, Levit. 19 31. & 20.6.

8. Is *Doreshel-hammathim*, Deut. 18.11. *Consulens mortuos*, a Necromancer, one that consults with the dead, Isa. 8.19. to know what he would desire of them. To which perhaps may allude that supposed speaking of Dives, of one rising from the dead to tell his brethren what they should do, Luk 16.

9. Are *Haittim*, Isa. 19.3. of At Linetudo, such as whisper with secret and soft words, as our white Witches do, in endeavoring to help man or beast. To these the Egyptians sought, as they did to their Idols, as the Prophet shows.[*] These are by us translated, Charmers.

10. Are *Chartummim*, Exo. 7.11. Some do call them Jugglers, deceivers, beguiling the sight: some hold them to be casters of Nativities,[†] Genethliac;[‡] which tell people their fortune, by the time of their birth: and they are called *Chartummim*, from their making of circles, and Characters: being compounded of *Cheret, calamus*, a quill or pen, & *Ataman, clausit*, shut up. These are only the names expressed in the Hebrew tongue, in all the old Testament, which set

[*] Isa. 19.3.
[†] P. de Loier de spectris, c. 12.
[‡] A calculator of nativities.

out rather good Witches, then these cursing bad Witches, which none can abide, but such as be of their society.

In the new testament we find, only the word Magus,[*] a Magician, Act. 8. The *Septuagints* translate the Hebrew words by diverse Greek words,[†] to set out rather the good, than bad witch. As *Cledomizomenos* from his same: another *Apophthegnomenos* for his short and sententious speaking: [‡] another *Ornithescopos*, because he foretold things by flying of birds: another *Eggastromuthus*, one speaking out of the belly: another *Gnostis* from knowledge, a Diviner. So that all the names of Hebrew and Greek in the old and new Testament, run upon such Witches, as the world doth follow after, rather than upon this hurting, and cursing, which I note not, as if these could do no harm, but,

1. To show how cross God is, in his judgment and condemnation of Witches, from the common course of men, who wholly, and only fly upon the black Witches, hunt them, imprison them, and hang them (as they deserve well) but they can pass by these white Witches, whom the holy Scriptures do so decipher to us, and condemn. These they can countenance and maintain: because these can satisfy their vain curiosities, their inquisitive natures, idle

---

[*] [Greek omitted]. Artem magicam exercens. (Exercising the art of magic)

[†] 2. Chron. 33. 6. Mich. 5.6. Levit. 19.26. & 19.31. 1 Sam. 28.3, 9.

[‡] 2 Kin. 21.6.

fantasies; yea and sometimes their mischievous purposes: but the end of such courses will be bitter: let Saul and *Manasseh* be a warning to all this kind.

2. To manifest the bloody malice of Satan in these latter times against mankind, who has stirred up such cruel Witches, as be wholly upon revenge, tormenting men, and women, and their cattle, making a trade of killing and murdering, of which sort the Scriptures hardly give an instance, except it be in *Balaam* hired to curse God's people. It may be, others could and did mischief: but it cannot be concluded, either from the instances of examples, or from their names, except, perhaps, somewhere the Septuagint do use the word *Pharmacos*,* which yet is used, as well in the better, as in the worse sense.

Let us therefore learn to follow the Lord, hate Witches, Wizards, Magicians, Soothsayers, Fortune-tellers, Astrologists, Enchanters, Juggling companions, dealing with Sorcery and Witchcraft.

1. For the great dishonor offered to God by these hellish miscreants, in the entrance, in the practice, and end of their devilish Arts.

2. In conscience to God's commandment, utterly forbidding to regard such, Levit. 19.31. for it is spiritual whoredom, and defilement, Levit. 20.6.

---

* Latin: drugs. Note the similarity to pharmacy.

3. Because such as used them first, were Heathen, as Egyptians, Canaanites, Philistines & Chaldeans: such as in Israel followed the heathenish customs, were wicked and ungodly: as Saul, who was a murderer, 1. Sam. 22. a profane neglecter of God's worship, 1. Chron. 13.3. and one whom God had forsaken had taken his spirit from, 1. Sa. 16.14. an evil spirit was upon him, to whom God vouchsafed* no answer by sacred means, 1. Sam. 28.16. and therefore, he fell to Witches. And what was *Manasseh*, but an Idolater, and an observer of times, & so fell to Witchery, and to such as had familiars? And the people which delighted in these, were haters of the true Teachers, and believed false prophets, Dreamers, and Diviners, Jerem. 27.9. And with us, what are they which regard these sorts, but either superstitious Papists, or Neutrals, or Atheists?

4. The evil which in the end will ensue to such as hearken to these;† what got *Saul* by going to them? They may soothe up for a time these vain persons, but at length the Devil will pay them home: Examples abroad, and in Histories, and within ourselves observed, may terrify all good Christians from seeking unto, and regarding of such. For its plainly said, that the Lord sets his face against such, to cut them off, Luk. 20.6. And if God be against them, what may they look for in the end?

---

* To grant or privilege special behavior
† *Delrio*, l. 6. pag. 1042. *monit*. 3. & 4

# CHAP. XXI.

## *That all sorts of Witches ought to die, even because they be Witches.*

There ought no such distinction of Witches to be made into good and bad,[*] blessing and cursing, white and black Witches, as thereby either sort should escape death. They may differ in name, but al are abomination to the Lord, and ought to dye.

[†]1. The Law of God says, without exception; *Thou shalt not suffer a Witch to live*. If a Witch, justly convicted, death is due to such a one.

2. They all make a league with the Devil: an act so execrable, to renounce God, and to betake themselves to the devil, as for this thing only they deserve death in the highest degree.

[‡] 3. For these abominations, the Lord utterly destroyed the Canaanites, Deut. 18.12. and plagued *Manasseh*, 2. Chron. 33.6. which wickedness of his was so abhorred of God, as in his displeasure he mentioned it many years after by Jeremy, as a cause

---

[*] *Delrio, lib*. 5. s. 16. pag 775, 776, 777.

[†] Exod. 22.18. Levit. 20 27.

[‡] *Delrio, lib*. 6. pag. 1042.

of removing the Jews from their land, and of leading them away captive into a strange land, Jer. 15.4.

4. Idolaters ought to dye, Exod. 22.20. & 32.28, 29. and enticers to Idolatry, Deut. 13.9. because they worship Devils, Psal. 106.37.1. Cor. 10.20. Rev. 9.20.[*] But Witches worship devils, they invocate them, crave help of them, work by them, and pay them homage, sacrifice to them, and they do it not to stocks and stones so mediately to the Devil, as other Idolaters do, but immediately to the very devil himself. And therefore, are the greatest Idolaters that can be, and so most worthy of death.

It will be granted that bad Witches ought to die, as being guilty some of murder,[†] other some of committing filthiness with Devils, by the confession of innumerable Witches; and for much mischief, and manifold harms which they do.

But still some doubt of so round dealing with the white Witches, which cure folk, & do as they imagine great good, tell wonders, and delight their hearers, & sometimes their beholders.

The imagined good Witches, the Conjurer, Enchanter, Magician, Soothsayer, and the rest ought to dye; for besides the former reasons;

---

[*] *Delrio, lib*. 5. *sec* 4. pa. 719.

[†] *Incubi, Succubi.*

1. As has been proved; the course of the Scriptures is generally against these.

2. *Saul* and *Josias* put these sorts to death, 1. Sa. 28.2. Kin. 23.24.[*] and King James in his book[†] says of Magicians and Necromancers, that they ought to be dealt with, as Sorcerers.

[‡]3. In other Countries such have been put to death. In Flanders was there a Magician, which by curing many diseases became famous, and was reputed a holy man, covering his Witchery, with appointing people to fast, to say their Pater noster, & to go on Pilgrimage to this or that Saint, but his Magick practices being found out, he had his desert.[§] In France there was a woman Witch, which did cure some with a pretended medicine, and by saying these words, *In the name of the Father, and of the Son, and of the holy Ghost, & of St. Anthony, and St. Michael, thou may be cured of thy disease, commending withal the party to hear Mass nine days*: but for all this, she had judgment to be burnt for her Witchcraft.

For these healers are oftentimes hurting Witches withal, and all healers do entice people from God, in requiring faith of them, & do cause the people to run a whoring after them, as *Moses* speaks, Lev. 20.6. Being therefore in league with Satan, being

---

[*] In his *Daemono*. l. 1. c. 7.

[†] Daemonologie (1591)

[‡] *Bodin. Daemo lib.* 3 c. 2.

[§] Lib. 3. cap.5.

abominable Idolaters, enticing people from their faith in God, they are worthy to die.

*4. Very Heathen Emperors have put to death such as were Necromancers, such as used to cure diseases, such as would undertake to foretell success of wars, & such have bin exiled, if not put to death, as would by Art. Magick; discover them, see examples of these in Bodin's *Daemonomania*.†

They offend then that countenance them, that prevent their apprehension, their judgment, and just deserved punishment.

---

* See Master *Roberts* his Treatise of Witchcraft, from pag. 75. to the end.
† *Bodin. lib. c.* 1. & 5. & l. 44. cap. 5. *Delrio, lib.* 5. *sec.* 4. p. 719, 720, 721.

# CHAP. XXII.

*That the bad Witches in their trial, persecution, conviction, and condemnation, should be dealt with, as is befitting, in the course of Justice.*

IT is miserable to behold how maliciously, how ragingly, in bitterness of spirit, the rude headless multitude, and other vain people cry out against these sorts of wretched Caitiffs, saying, eye upon them, Away with them, Hang them, and some of them stick not to curse them. A brutish and unchristianly carriage.

It is true that their sin is very grievous, hateful to God, and to be detested of all true Christians, as an execrable falling from God, into the deepest service of the devil: but yet let men consider:

1. A difference between their fearful sin, and their persons; hate the one, but not the other.

2. That Satan is a powerful Deceiver, and Seducer, who can make an *Eve* in Paradise, (being in the state of perfection) to believe him, the Devil, before God.

3. That by nature corrupt, we are no less apt to be misled by him, [*] then they; walking in sins and trespasses, according to the course of the world, and according to the Prince of darkness, in inordinate affection, and other lusts, being foolish, disobedient,[†] deceived, serving diverse lusts & pleasures, living in malice, envy, hateful, and hating one another. Thus, by nature are we the children of wrath, and bemired with the filth of sin, as well as they.

4. That therefore our difference arises not, from within ourselves, as from our own wisdom, will and power: but we are kept from their Apostasy, either by God's restraining power: as he kept the King of *Gerar Abimelech* from *Adultery*: as also *Pharaoh* from *Abraham's* wife: or by his converting grace; so everyone must say with Saint *Paul*: *By the grace of God, I am that I am.*[‡]

5. Consider, that some so dreadfully caught by Satan, may be God's servants, and be converted; as was *Manasseh*, and also *Saint Cyprian*, of whom before. And did not such as used curious Arts, even Magick, turn to God and believe?

Therefore let us behold in them a spectacle of man's misery, as being left of God unto the power of the Devil, and so be moved with compassion, to pray for

---

[*] Ephes. 2.1, 2. Col. 3.3, 7.

[†] Titus 3.3. Ephes. 2.

[‡] When God commanded Moses to speak with the Israelite elders in Egypt, Moses asked the name of the god which sent him, which God replied 'I am who I am' from Exodus 3:14.

their conversion. In ourselves preserved, behold the merciful goodness of our God, and so be stirred up to praise his name. Thus, shall we make a good use of both, and behave ourselves as sober Christians ought to do.

# CHAP. XXIII.

## *Satan strives to imitate God, in whatsoever he may, as far as God will permit him.*

Many things may seem very strange, and hardly to be believed, which are related to be done between the Devil and Witches. But all this will seem no wonder, if men do wisely consider, that Satan endeavors to be an imitator of God, not to please him, but rather to cross him, and to beguile these hellish Apostates, and to increase the more their sins, and just condemnation.

## *Behold, What the Lord does:*

1. The Lord has his set Assemblies for his servants to meet together.

2. The Lord has his Sabbaths.

3. The Lord has visible Congregation which consist of good and bad persons, learned and unlearned, but of these the last are the most.

4. Amongst these is the use of Baptism, where they give to the baptized a name.

5. The Lord makes a Covenant with his people, and they with him.

6. The Lord confirmed his covenant with blood.

7. The Lord marks his.

8. The Lord gives to those that are his, his Spirit and gifts withal.

9. These do honor the Lord and worship him.

10. These call upon the Lord, when they would have his help.

11. The Lord had some which wrought by his power, though they by open profession did not follow him.

12. The Lord requires faith of such as seek to him for help.

13. The Lord had such as by words cured diseases, by prayer, and did anoint the party infirm: so by some things brought them from the sick, and carried to the sick again, Jam. 5. Mark. 6.13. Act. 19.12.

14. The Lord by his servant raised some from the dead, 1. King. 17.21. Act. 9 40.

15. The Lord had such as freely used their gift of healing, Mat. 10.8.

16. The Lord had some, which by cursing and threatening procured evil upon others, 2. King. 2.24. Act. 13.

17. The Lord tied his to certain rules, & ordinances in his service, and sometimes to a certain number, Jos. 6.15.1. Kin. 17.21.

18. The Lord makes some to be his, either by his own immediate inspiration, and speaking to them, or wins them to him by his instruments.

19. The Lord appointed some burnt offering for atonement, and so to free his from some evils.

20. In the Scripture is found the cutting of hair & burning it, Num. 6.18. the writing of words, and the blotting of them out a gain, and to give them unto one, Num. 5.23. also, the giving of a potion. Num. 5.27.

21. The Lord cast some of his into trances, in which they saw many things, and seemed to be in other places, Ezek. 3. 14. and 12. 1. 24. and 40. 2. Rev. 1. 22.

22. The Lord would take some of his, and suddenly carry them from one place to another bodily, Act. 8.39.

23. The Lord had such as could tell of things past, things present, but hidden, and of things to come.

24. In the Scripture is told of curing one disease, and the same to fall upon another. 2. Ki. 5.27.

25. The Lord had such as could work miracles & strange wonders.

26. The Lord by his heavenly work moves men to holy actions, as preparative to further them to a better knowledge of him; when he shall be pleased further to reveal himself, Act. 8.28.

27. The Lord spoke by a beast unto a Witch, Num. 22.28.

28. The Lord ordained sacrifices to be offered unto him.

29. The Lord has promised earthly blessings, to stir up people to serve him.

## Behold, What Satan does:

1. So the Devil has his set meetings for his Magicians and Witches to come together.

2. So Satan with his Witches have their times, which they call their Sabbaths.

3. So the meetings of these are of good and bad Witches, some learned, and some ignorant, but of these the greatest number.

4. So it is amongst these; for they meet to christen (as they speak) their spirits, and give them names.

5. So doth Satan and the Witches covenant one with the other.

6. So doth Satan ratify his covenant with blood.

7. So Satan marks his.

8. So Satan gives to his a Familiar or Spirit, and gifts to do this or that trick of Witchcraft.

9. So these pay homage to Satan, and worship him.

10. So when these would have help, they call upon their Spirit, or Devil.

11. So Satan has some which work by his power, though they make no open or express league with him.

12. So doth Satan by his instruments require says of such as come to him for help.

13. So has Satan such as seem by words to cure diseases, so by forms of prayers and by oils: also by bringing something from the sick party, and carrying the same back again.

14. So Satan makes show by his servants to raise up the dead, 1. Sam. 28.

15. So will the Devil have such as shall profess to cure for nothing.

16. So Satan has such, which by cursing & threats procure mischief to others.

17. So Satan ties his Witches to certain words and deeds in going about his service, & to observe numbers, to do a thing so & so often, 3. times, 7. times, etc.

18. So Satan makes some Witches by inward suggestions, & his speaking to them, or by using other Witches to gain them to him.

19. So Satan has taught his to burn something (as a sacrifice to him for an atonement) to free the bewitched from pain.

20. So Satan teaches his to cut off hair, and burn it, & to write a charm and blot it out, and then give it one, also to use potions; thus seeming by these imitations to have Scriptures or warrant.

21. So the Devil casts some of his into trances, in which they seem to themselves to be in other places: where they verily believe that they see and do many things.

22. So Satan will take some of his, and carry them bodily from one place to another, *Del. de disq. Mag.* l. 2 q. 16 & l. 5. s. 16. p. 760.

23. So Satan has his, whom he teaches to tell of all these sorts of things.

24. So we may find how, when a disease is cured by a Witch, it is transferred sometime upon another person or creature.

25. So Satan has his Magicians and Sorcerers, to work wonders, Exo. 7.

26. So Satan by his hellish suggestions and operation, stirs up people to think of, plot and purpose evils; so preparing them for himself, to accept of his counsel when he appears to them.

27. So Satan speaks to witches sometimes in forms of beasts, & sometimes in the very creatures themselves.

28. So Satan has taught his to offer sacrifice, Num. 23.

29. So Satan promises such things to Witches, as Motives to serve him, Mat. 4.

Thus we see in these few things, how Satan observes the Lords doings and sayings, and therein strives to be like him. The truth of these things on God's part is evident out of the holy Scripture: on Satan's part the truth is set out before in these two books confirmed by many testimonies in the Margin everywhere.

The end of publishing these (not hitherto set forth by any) is to show some ground of those things which we find related in the writings of men, and to be done between Witches and Devils, which otherwise may seem to be beyond all credit, and to be rejected as fabulous; which if *Wierus, Scot* and others had known, & diligently weighed, they had not so lightly esteemed of the true relations of learned men, and imputed the strange actions, undoubtedly done by Witches, and Devils, only to brainsick Conceits, and mad Melancholy.

FINIS.

22903711R00118

Printed in Great Britain
by Amazon